Service Learning
for Youth Empowerment
and Social Change

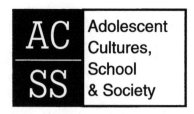

AC / SS
Adolescent Cultures, School & Society

Joseph L. DeVitis & Linda Irwin-DeVitis
General Editors

Vol. 5

PETER LANG
New York • Washington, D.C./Baltimore • Boston
Bern • Frankfurt am Main • Berlin • Vienna • Paris

Service Learning
for Youth Empowerment
and Social Change

Edited by
Jeff Claus and Curtis Ogden

PETER LANG
New York • Washington, D.C./Baltimore • Boston
Bern • Frankfurt am Main • Berlin • Vienna • Paris

Library of Congress Cataloging-in-Publication Data

Service learning for youth empowerment and social change /
[edited by] Jeff Claus and Curtis Ogden.
p. cm. — (Adolescent cultures, school, and society; vol. 5)
Includes bibliographical references and index.
1. Student service—United States. I. Claus, Jeff. II. Ogden, Curtis.
III. Series: Adolescent cultures, school & society; vol. 5.
LC220.5.S458   370.11'5—dc21   98-37904
ISBN 0-8204-3858-8
ISSN 1091-1464

Die Deutsche Bibliothek-CIP-Einheitsaufnahme

Service learning for youth empowerment and social change /
ed. by Jeff Claus and Curtis Ogden. –New York; Washington, D.C./Baltimore;
Boston; Bern; Frankfurt am Main; Berlin; Vienna; Paris: Lang.
(Adolescent cultures, school and society; Vol. 5)
ISBN 0-8204-3858-8

Cover design by David Hyman

The paper in this book meets the guidelines for permanence and durability
of the Committee on Production Guidelines for Book Longevity
of the Council of Library Resources.

© 1999, 2001, 2004 Peter Lang Publishing, Inc., New York

Printed in the United States of America

For my parents,
who have taught me much, by example,
about the value and rewards of service;
and for Judy.

Jeff Claus

For my mother and father,
thank you for the constant encouragement;
and for the many teachers in my life
who helped shape my passion and purpose.

Curtis Ogden

And with great respect and admiration
for the Learning Web,
a youth service organization in Ithaca, New York,
and for all the young people
who have so many times inspired us with
their commitment to caring, justice, and action.

Contents

Contributors

Tricia Bowers-Young is Director of Moving in the Spirit, a dance troupe/service program in Atlanta, Georgia, in which youth choreograph and perform to address themes of social justice and contemporary issues in their community. They perform locally, nationally, and abroad.

Richard J. Clark, Jr., is Dean of the College of Education at the University of Massachusetts Boston, and is former director of 180 Days in Springfield, a community service/teacher education initiative in Springfield, Massachusetts.

Jeff Claus is an Assistant Professor with the Center for Teacher Education, Ithaca College, Ithaca, New York. During 1992–94 he was coordinator and developer of a community service program at the Learning Web, a youth service organization in Ithaca. He has conducted research and published articles on service learning, youth employment programs, vocational education, and critical theories of schooling in the United States. Most recently, he coauthored, "Reflection as a Natural Element of Service: Service Learning for Youth Empowerment," published in *Equity and Excellence in Education.*

Joy DesMarais is a senior at the College of St. Catherine in St. Paul, Minnesota, and is coordinator of strategic youth initiatives at the National Youth Leadership Council, where she provides training and technical assistance for young people and adults involved in service learning and other youth initiatives. As a senior in high school she founded a youth-led performance group, The Troupe, which uses improvisational drama to educate young people about critical health issues and decision making.

Alice L. Halsted is President of the National Helpers Network. She leads national dissemination efforts for the Network, working to establish service-learning programs based on the Early Adolescent Helper Program model throughout the country. She is author of numerous articles on service learning that have appeared in *Phi Delta Kappan, The New England Journal of Public Policy, The Middle School Journal, and Midpoints.* She is also coauthor of *Standards for School-Based Service Learning,* with Joan Schine, and has served as a national invitee to the President's Summit on Service.

Joseph Kahne is an Assistant Professor in the College of Education at the University of Illinois at Chicago and is Codirector of the Chicago Network of Service Learning and Democratic Citizenship. He works with schools and community organizations on the design, implementation, and evaluation of service-learning initiatives. His research and writing focus on service learning, democracy, and educational policy. His most recent book, *Reframing Educational Policy: Democracy, Community, and the Individual,* was published in 1996.

Carol Kinsley is Executive Director of the Community Service Learning Center in Springfield, Massachusetts, and Adjunct Professor in the School of Education, University of Massachusetts at Amherst. She has published articles about community service in *Phi Delta Kappan, Community Education Journal,* and *Equity and Excellence in Education.*

Richard D. Lakes is Associate Professor in the Department of Educational Policy Studies at Georgia State University. He edited and contributed to the book *Critical Education for Work* and is the author of the recently published *Youth Development and Critical Education: The Promise of Democratic Action,* a book about community service programs.

Irene S. LaRoche is a graduate student at the University of Massachusetts and Recruitment Coordinator for 180 Days in Springfield, a teacher education/community service initiative in Springfield, Massachusetts.

Robert W. Maloy is a Lecturer in the School of Education at the University of Massachusetts at Amherst and is Codirector of 180 Days in Springfield, a community service/teacher education initiative in

Springfield, Massachusetts. Most recently, he is coauthor of the book *Schools for an Information Age* and of "Learning through Community Service Is Political," an article in *Equity and Excellence in Education.*

Curtis Ogden is coordinator of a community service program, ImPACT, run by the Learning Web, a community-based youth service organization in Ithaca, New York. He has published a number of articles on service learning, community development, and youth empowerment, most recently coauthoring "Reflection as a Natural Element of Service: Service Learning for Youth Empowerment" in *Equity and Excellence in Education.* He has also done community development work in southern Africa.

Cynthia Parsons, a former education editor of the *Christian Science Monitor,* is currently director of SerVermont, a nationally recognized service-learning initiative. She has published numerous articles on community service programs in such journals as *Phi Delta Kappan* and *Equity and Excellence in Education* and is the author of the recently published book *Community Service Learning: A Guide to Including Service in the Public School Curriculum.*

Joan Schine was founding Director of the National Center for Service Learning in Early Adolescence and is now a private consultant. Her most recent publication about community service is as a contributor to and editor of the 1997 book *Service Learning.*

Abbie Sheehan is a middle-school teacher at the Chestnut Accelerated Middle School for the Visual and Performing Arts in Springfield, Massachusetts.

Joel Westheimer is an Assistant Professor in the Department of Teaching and Learning and a fellow in the Center for the Study of American Culture and Education at New York University. A former New York City public school teacher, he currently works with schools on the design, implementation, and evaluation of service-learning and experience-based curriculum. His research and writing focus on service learning, democracy, and the development of teachers' professional community. His most recent book is *Among Schoolteachers: Community, Autonomy, and Ideology in Teachers' Work.*

Miranda Yates is a project director at the Menninger Foundation's Center for Outcome Research and Effectiveness. Her research focuses on identity formation and social development in adolescents. With James Youniss, she has published writings about the roots of civic engagement and social responsibility, including the recent book *Community Service and Social Responsibility in Youth.*

James Youniss is Director of the Life Cycle Institute and Professor of psychology at the Catholic University of America. He studies social-moral development in children and youth and has a special interest in the role of culture, including religion and politics, in development. He is coauthor, with Miranda Yates, of the recent book *Community Service and Social Responsibility in Youth.*

Chapter 1

Service Learning for Youth Empowerment and Social Change: An Introduction

Jeff Claus and Curtis Ogden

It is clear from recent publications, conferences, legislation, and trends in funding that the idea of engaging youth in educationally framed community service activity is now a full-fledged movement. For those of us who believe this kind of experience, often referred to as *service learning*, represents an important direction in the pursuit of educational and social reform, this is an exciting time. Community service learning is increasingly recognized as a valuable way to make education and learning more relevant and meaningful to the lives of youth, and it is understood to close the gap that so often exists between schools and their communities. It can provide young people with an opportunity to learn about and address significant real world issues in responsible ways, and it can contribute to the development of an improved sense of community, both among the youth involved and within the communities served. Service experience, when set in a framework of substantive reflection, can also motivate and empower young people to think critically about their world and to act on it with a growing sense of purpose, agency, and optimism. In this way, service learning promises constructive youth development, as it contributes to a clearer sense of identity, self-worth, efficacy, and belonging, and it can motivate and prepare young people to work for valuable social change. In the process, it has the potential to serve as a strong antidote to the disconnectedness so often associated with adolescence in the postmodern world.

There is a risk, however, that service learning will become a somewhat superficial or "feel good" addition to the regular offerings of schools and agencies rather than an informed effort to help youth develop skills fundamental to the democratic pursuit of social change. A number of us interested in service learning have expressed this concern recently (Boyte, 1991; Jones, Maloy, and Steen, 1996; Kahne and Westheimer, 1996; Karp, 1997; Lakes, 1996; Ogden and Claus, 1997), and this book is an attempt to address the issue further and offer solutions. The intent of this book is to provide theory and practice, guidance and inspiration, based on the perspectives of academic researchers, service-learning practitioners, and youth participants, in support of developing service-learning programs that will educate and empower young people to question, learn about, act on, and contribute to the improvement of our complex and often alienating world. It is our hope that the voices presented here will encourage us all toward a service learning that contributes to both constructive youth development *and* educational and social reform. In our view these objectives are highly interwoven, mutually inclusive elements of a single whole.

Early in our work soliciting contributions for this book we contacted Dorothy Stoneman, director of YouthBuild USA, a wonderful national program that engages young people in housing rehabilitation and other community improvement projects. The emphasis in this program is on "helping young people take charge of their own lives and become effective and ethical young leaders committed to the well being of their community and the world" (Stoneman, 1993, preface). Ultimately, Ms. Stoneman was too busy to contribute a chapter, but as one who is wise about youth, community needs, and issues of social justice, she made a significant contribution in conversation. In one of our discussions with her about what we hoped to accomplish in the book, she explained that the focus of her work, and the work of youth in the YouthBuild programs, is not service but rather the development of leadership skills and the pursuit of action leading to community improvement. She made it clear that while service may be a part of what young people in YouthBuild do, the emphasis is on creating opportunities for and education in youth leadership and activism.

We think this distinction is an important one. It is easy for service programs to become focused on altruism and acts of goodwill determined primarily by adults, in which those providing the service feel good about themselves for having done something for others less fortunate. While this is certainly well intentioned, and it may sometimes lead to learning about self and society, it often leaves unturned fertile opportunities to engage youth in investigating and reflecting on their own lives and the roots of the circumstances they address. It also often neglects the potential of service to educate and empower youth to act on their world for the purpose of improving it. This, we feel, is a crucial point. The power of service learning resides not only in its experiential and humanitarian nature but in its participatory and problem-posing potential. The degree to which young people engage in the processes of exploring, analyzing, critiquing, suggesting, deciding, planning, and acting through service greatly determines the impact of the experience on their understanding of themselves and their surroundings. We like to think that service learning can provide powerful opportunities for youth to reflect critically and constructively on their world and to develop skills for facilitating meaningful social change.

The chapters in this book present both rationale and examples in support of this view. In the opening chapter Joan Schine explains why we should value service learning, especially given the current call for more tests and standards. She argues that service learning can integrate cognitive and affective development, prepare youth for both workplace success and democratic participation, and foster individual growth and a greater sense of mutual respect and community commitment. In the process, she suggests, it can foster deeper understanding than much traditional instruction, and it can counteract the sense of hopelessness many young people feel as they begin, in their early adolescence, to engage the adult world. She outlines features of service learning that can give it this kind of power, and she encourages educators, policy makers, and citizens to value a more integrated, holistic approach to learning and development.

Adding to these ideas, Joe Kahne and Joel Westheimer address the critical and too often unconsidered question of what the goal or purpose of service learning should be. They present analysis and discussion of the recent history of the movement and of research they have conducted with 24 K–12 teachers involved in running service projects. They conclude that service learning should help students go beyond acts of "charity" to develop the skills and perspectives of critical reflection and action central to the pursuit of constructive social change. In support of this point, they provide examples of different kinds of service experience, paying particular attention to demonstrating what they mean by a "strong" version of service. This sets an excellent standard that many of us may not yet achieve but that can and should guide our program design and service-learning efforts.

The book then moves on to more specific program descriptions and analyses. Miranda Yates and Jim Youniss discuss an effective urban high school service program in which students work in a soup kitchen as part of a course on social justice. Drawing on theories of adolescent development and extensive reports by the students in journals, interviews, and reflection sessions, Yates and Youniss demonstrate how the experience of working in the soup kitchen, when combined with the richly reflective framework of the course, positively influences the students' sense of identity and social justice. Yates and Youniss argue and illustrate that the reflective framework is critical, and they identify and discuss features of the course central to its success.

In chapter 5 we (Claus and Ogden) discuss our experiences designing and running a service program over the last five years and explain how we have grown to value key concepts from Ira Shor's book *Empowering Education: Critical Teaching for Social Change* (1992). We present these concepts and explain how they have led us to create a program in which participants have responsibility for determining and carrying out their own group-run projects. Specifically, we describe our work with youth to define "community" and "service," investigate and analyze the community, learn about and employ democratic process, and reflect critically and act on the world around us. The process is as important as the product, and the focus is on engaging in thoughtful community action that will empower young people to care, question, and act in their lives beyond the program.

Alice Halsted also writes about a program, Community Problem Solvers, in which service is viewed as community action and young people identify and work together on their own group projects. This program, developed by the National Helpers Network, is designed for early adolescents and shows how with good planning, consisting of a combination of structure and flexibility, this age group can be guided productively into reflective and empowering community-based learning and action.

Tricia Bowers-Young and Rick Lakes describe in their chapter a community- and arts-based service program in Atlanta called Moving in the Spirit. In this program youth choreograph and perform dances around community issues and themes of social justice for the purpose of educating and generating productive discussion with their audiences. Reports by youth in the program show the value and power of providing young people with opportunities and guidance for addressing critical community issues in creative and meaningful ways.

Joy DesMarais then reflects on her experience starting and working in a high school service group in which young people use improvisational drama to educate their peers about a number of critical social and health issues. She discusses the positive effects of this experience on her development, and she describes how she now wants to bring this kind of service learning to others. She also presents ideas for how adults and young people can work effectively together to ensure that youth have substantial leadership roles in service programs.

Cynthia Parsons continues this theme, writing broadly about the need for our schools to create opportunities for young people to *practice* democracy rather than just study it. Service learning and the critical thought and action it can promote will, she argues, contribute to the development of a literacy for participatory democracy.

Next there are two chapters that address the need to prepare new teachers as effective leaders of service-learning projects. Both chapters present research and discussion of initiatives at the University of Massachusetts, Amherst, in which teacher education students are engaged as service-learning leaders and aides. Robert Maloy, Abbie Sheehan, Irene LaRoche, and Richard Clark write that the activist nature of some of the projects they studied created a relevance and purposefulness that was exciting to both the teachers and students and led to substantive reflection about critical social issues. Carol Kinsley, drawing on rich reflective material from teacher education students, demonstrates that the service-learning experience helped preservice teachers better understand the complexity of the educational project and the value of making meaningful connections with the community. Even though the two chapters address different programs, they both show how involvement in service learning can increase teacher education students' confidence and skill with an active, student-centered, reflective pedagogy. In this way they demonstrate the value of incorporating service learning into teacher preparation programs, as this seems to promote much in the way of effective teaching and constructive school reform.

In the final chapter of the book, Curtis Ogden poses some critical questions about how we define and employ the concept of service. Answers to these questions, he argues, have implications for the future of the service-learning movement and its potential to achieve equitable social change. He especially cautions us against allowing service to become a one-way act in which our primary concern is the experience or development of "those providing the service." Instead, he suggests, we need to move beyond conventional notions of service to a broader vision that focuses on just and sustainable community development achieved through reflection and democratic action.

It is our hope that the issues and ideas presented in these chapters will further understanding and appreciation of the role service learning can play in the pursuit of substantive youth development and social change. We acknowledge that service learning has the potential to invigorate schools by creating vital connections between curricula and communities. It can also initiate students into important work on behalf of others. However, if service learning is to live up to its full potential of helping us address the needs of our increasingly fractured world, we must embrace it as democratic, reflective community action. This means aspiring to greater depths in program design and facilitation, with particular attention paid to some of the key ideas presented in this book. We encourage the reader to proceed with enthusiasm in the project of creating a deeper and more complex approach to service learning.

References

Boyte, H. 1991. Community service and civic education. *Phi Delta Kappan,* 72: 765–767.

Jones, B., R. Maloy, and C. Steen. 1996. Learning through community service is political. *Equity and Excellence in Education,* 29(2): 37–45.

Kahne, J., and J. Westheimer. 1996. In the service of what? The politics of service learning. *Phi Delta Kappan,* 77: 593–599.

Karp, S. 1997. Educating for a civil society: The core issue is inequality. *Educational Leadership,* 54: 40–43.

Lakes, R. 1996. *Youth development and critical education: The promise of democratic action.* Albany, N.Y.: SUNY Press.

Ogden, C., and J. Claus. 1997. Reflection as a natural element of service: Service learning for youth empowerment. *Equity and Excellence in Education,* 30(1): 72–81.

Shor, I. 1992. *Empowering education: Critical teaching for social change.* Chicago: University of Chicago Press.

Stoneman, D. 1993. *Leadership development: A handbook from youthbuild USA and the youth action program.* Somerville, Mass.: YouthBuild USA.

Chapter 2

Beyond Test Scores and Standards: Service, Understanding, and Citizenship

Joan Schine

[T]he shaping of civility in a context of democratic social and political civitas will not be advanced by a system of schooling geared primarily to economic ends.
—John Goodlad, "On Shifting Reform Debate from Utility to Humanity"

A Nation at Risk, the 1983 report of the National Commission on Excellence in Education, is frequently regarded as the wake-up call that gave rise to much of the furor over education reform, national standards, and standardized tests.

> Our Nation is at risk. Our once unchallenged preeminence in commerce, industry, science, and technological innovation is being overtaken by competitors throughout the world. . . . [T]he educational foundations of our society are presently being eroded by a rising tide of mediocrity that threatens our very future as a Nation and a people. What was unimaginable a generation ago has begun to occur—others are matching and surpassing our educational attainments. . . . We have, in effect, been committing an act of unthinking, unilateral educational disarmament. (National Commission on Excellence in Education, 1983, 5)

It is worth noting that the alarm was sounded largely in terms of winning and losing, in the language of combat, even of weapons, and of international competition rather than of social benefit or human potential. It is that perspective that, more than a decade later, still informs much of the support for national testing and "tough" academic standards.

Few, if any, observers of public education in this country express wholehearted satisfaction with the current state of affairs. "Reform" efforts proliferate, their number surpassed only by critical commentaries from both the left and the right, from educators themselves and from every sector of the public.

At least as persistent as allegations that the schools are failing to prepare the workers that our economy requires are accusations of academic deficiency. Much of the support for more rigorous standards and universal testing has developed as a response to these concerns. Critics also charge that the schools of the nineties have abdicated their responsibility to transmit the society's "core values" to the next generation. This is an issue not well addressed by the establishment of standards, as it is difficult to assess or measure progress in this area. One would be hard put, for example, to devise a standardized test of growth in citizenship or altruism. This may account for the absence of any data concerning citizenship in the 1997 National Goals Report, *Building a Nation of Learners*, although the third goal of the eight identified by the National Goals Panel is titled "Student Achievement and Citizenship." (An earlier panel report cited voter registration as the single measure of achievement in the area of citizenship.)

It is entirely reasonable to expect our schools to enable students to master the knowledge and skills they will need as workers and citizens. And it is reasonable, too, to hold schools accountable for meeting this goal. Supporters of national standards maintain that standards that state clearly what children "should know and be able to do" at various grade levels are necessary if we are to be able to judge the school's success. They assert further that high expectations are ordinarily a precursor of high achievement and, therefore, that the establishment of rigorous standards will lead to improved learning.

No one would question that it is in the national interest to have an educated citizenry, nor would we deny that citizens of the twenty-first century will need an education vastly different from our traditional notions of schooling. We can agree that literacy is the sine qua non for a productive life in the twenty-first century; basic math skills and some familiarity with literature and history are also generally accepted as components of a basic education; and "computer literacy" is the newest member of the family of "basic skills." There is also substantial popular support for the role of the school in teaching the skills of critical thinking and decision making, and polls indicate that virtually all of us believe that honesty and respect for the law, for the rights of others, and for property are among the "core values" that schools may properly convey. Like the support for demanding academic standards, the call for a curriculum component variously known as values education, ethics, citizenship, or character education comes not only from the education community but from parents and the public at large.

> The challenge to school reformers, whatever their special concern or remedy, is to bring into balance a wide range of interests and needs. They will need to move beyond the popular tendency to see cognitive and affective learning as competing areas to the goal of creating a learning environment where each enriches the other. Eric Schaps and his colleagues at the Developmental Studies Center in Oakland describe what they refer to as "two essential aspects of effective schooling." They are: "important and engaging learning opportunities" and "opportunities for membership in a caring community of learners." These elements, they assert, "are so strongly interdependent that each is actually indispensable to full realization of the other. . . . When a school community deliberately emphasizes the importance of learning *and* the importance of behaving humanely and responsibly, students have standards of competence and character to live and learn by" (Schaps, Battistich, and Solomon, 1987, 128–129).

Service Learning and the Mission of Public Education

Today's insistence on standards and national testing reflects the current support, from Washington to local PTAs, for a "get-tough" approach to curriculum and student achievement and for strict accountability. Many of the most vocal sponsors of rigorous academic standards for all students also contend that the mission of the school is diluted when social skills, multicultural education, or community participation are included in its offerings. On the other hand, some take the position that the key to school improvement lies in a total overhaul of the instructional program, with renewed emphasis on relevance and connecting classroom learning to "the real world." Others maintain that the central mission of the schools is the transmission of democratic values and the preparation of students for civic participation. Some proponents of this philosophy also hold that the school itself must first of all exemplify a democratic community, and all its activities (curriculum, staff development, classroom processes, governance) must flow from that center. And proponents of the "full-service school" maintain that health and social services for children, youth, and families should be located in the school and should be an integral part of the school itself. They argue that ease of access can greatly increase the likelihood of school success for those children who are most at risk.

Whereas schools once shared with other institutions and grassroots agencies a critical role in building community and bringing diverse constituencies together, there is today a loss of the sense of community, a fraying of the social fabric, and a growing isolation of youth. The role of the school as hub of the community is disappearing. The schools, like other sectors of the society, are today largely unable or unwilling to attempt to reverse that trend.

> The traditional community, whatever its shortcomings, did create, through the immediate family, through the extended family, and through all the interlocking networks of community life, a structure of social interdependency in which individuals gave and received support—all giving, all receiving. With that no longer available, we must seek to reconstruct comparable systems of dependable interdependency wherever we can—in the workplace, the church, the school, the youth-serving organizations. (Gardner, 1992, 4)

These diverse perspectives are often represented as mutually exclusive, and an artificial conflict is created. When cognitive and affective learning are seen as competing for a place in the school program, or when the school's role is narrowly defined as simply a purveyor of knowledge, the only real "loser" is the student. If our students are to be ready for the challenges of the next century, they will need a solid knowledge base and the skills that will enable them to continue to expand that knowledge. But at least as crucial for their success beyond the years of formal education will be an understanding of human behavior, of the interactions of groups, and of their own place in the society. As they reach the middle school and high school years, many young people have no vision of a personal future or any realization that they can take control of their own lives. The school, through programs such as service learning and civic education, can help these young people grow toward becoming active members of the society, "doer" rather than "done-to," toward a sense of themselves as potential change agents, able to make a difference.

There are those who argue that the business of education has been too broadly defined, that the task of the school is to prepare students for participation in the economy, and it ought not assume the burden of addressing the social and civic problems of our time. As we prepare to enter the new century, this argument is an anachronism. "Ought" or "ought not" is no longer the issue; the schools have no choice. They cannot effectively educate even those children who come to school ready to learn if a sizable minority of students have little or no personal stake in the society, lack social skills, and have few connections with adults who model positive behaviors, articulate expectations, and set standards for the young to meet.

Whatever one's bias, one cannot disagree with Jeremy Rifkin's statement that "The public schools are in trouble, and increasingly taxpayers are unwilling to support them." Rifkin goes on to suggest that the schools "need a new mission—one that prepares our children not only for the marketplace but also for their obligations to the civil society. Service learning will appeal to people because it both prepares children for adult responsibilities and helps to restore the civic life of the country" (Rifkin, 1996, 609).

The fact that service learning may appeal to taxpayers is not, however, sufficient reason for anointing it the "new mission" of the public schools. As frequently happens with a new program (or, as in the case of service learning, a revival of a program with roots in past practice), enthusiasts tend to present it as the new miracle drug, destined to address multiple needs and problems. As Harold Howe observed in 1972: "About every five years education in the United States finds a new rallying cry. Right after World War II 'life adjustment education' was emblazoned on the banner of school reformers. A similar notion . . . prospered in the colleges under the slogan of 'general education.' As these labels became dog-eared in the 1950s they were supplanted by new catchwords, each claiming to point to a new 'right' way for American teaching and learning" (Howe, 1972, 3).

These words of caution hold true today; there is still no single "quick fix" for the multitude of problems our schools and our young people must face. Nevertheless, in the mid-1990s, in meetings and conferences about school change and community involvement, it was almost inevitable that at some point a participant would suggest that service learning should be the cornerstone of school improvement—"the engine that drives school reform."

No Easy Answers

Committed though this writer is to the value of service learning, I would caution strongly against making overenthusiastic claims and inviting unrealistic expectations. Service learning is a promising endeavor—it embodies the principles enunciated by John Dewey as "learning by doing" and includes many of the elements found in curricula for character education, civics education, ethics, and similar programs—but it is not education's miracle drug. The impact of service learning has only fairly recently received serious attention from the research community, and although some preliminary findings have been published (e.g., Blyth and Scales, 1997), it is premature to draw broad conclusions. Because service learning can indeed be tailored to serve a variety of purposes, investigations focus on a range of "outcomes," including impact on academic achievement, social and psychological development, continuing commitment to community involvement, and attitude toward school and community.

Some advocates assert that in today's climate any addition to the existing program must enhance student achievement as measured against standards or by objective tests. And they say that unless it can be demonstrated that service learning contributes directly to academic success, it will simply be one more fragile "add-on," susceptible to the vicissitudes of schedules and discretionary funding. Teachers and administrators point out, too, that the schedule in most middle schools and high schools is already tightly packed; numbers of worthwhile programs and projects already compete for time. These arguments bring into sharp focus the challenge facing those who believe that schools must attend to affective as well as cognitive learning. Richard Kraft describes the dilemma:

> One of the major difficulties in evaluating or researching service-learning programs is the lack of agreement on what is meant by the term service learning and exactly what it is meant to accomplish. Whereas some programs emphasize social growth, character development, or civic responsibility, others attempt to study psychological development and effects of programs on self-concept. Moral judgment studies have sought to evaluate the effects of service on moral and ego development, and other studies have attempted to measure the effects of service on the broader community. Perhaps the most difficult arena has been in the area of intellectual, cognitive, and academic effects. It has been difficult to design tight experiments to isolate the effects of service on specific academic achievements. (Kraft, 1996, 142–143)

This is not to say that service learning has no place in the typical curriculum. On the contrary, there are countless examples of curricula that successfully include service learning in the traditional subject areas. A great many schools, and an even greater number of individual teachers, have successfully integrated service learning in the classroom and report heightened student interest when they are actively involved. This approach is not confined to any single discipline. Social studies classes may interview senior citizens as part of a unit on local history or work at a soup kitchen in connection with a study of world hunger.

The science class may undertake to clean up a local waterway or collect data on recycling or conservation on behalf of a municipal agency. A math class in one community designed a small nature walk on the school grounds, computing quantities of materials needed for the walks, topsoil, etc. Students in language arts classes have produced neighborhood newsletters, sometimes calling attention to local problems and proposing solutions; others have created storybooks around familiar local scenes for preschool children. No matter what the subject area, students can reinforce their own learning by teaching younger children or tutoring their peers.[1] Nevertheless, it may be difficult to demonstrate a cause-and-effect relationship between participation in service learning and improved academic performance.

Some students and parents, as well as a handful of policy makers, oppose school-based community service of any kind, labeling it "compulsory volunteering" or even "indentured servitude." But *Phi Delta Kappan's* annual Gallup poll has for several years found that a substantial majority of parents and the public support school-sponsored service, and several court challenges of service requirements have failed.

Chester Finn and Gregg Vanourek, scholars at the Hudson Institute in Indianapolis, characterize the endorsement of service learning in Goals 2000 as the endorsement of "mandatory volunteer work—an oxymoron known variously in the field as 'experiential education,' 'character education,' 'community service,' and, most frequently, 'service learning'" (Finn and Vanourek, 1995, 46). Not content with insisting that a service-learning requirement amounts to "mandatory voluntarism," Finn and Vanourek suggest that it "runs the risk of degrading the virtue of service itself, while politicizing the school curriculum and recruiting impressionable youths for causes dear to the hearts of graying activists" (1995, 48).

Although Finn and Vanourek are somewhat more strident in their denunciation than other critics, the controversy it represents is nothing new and will no doubt continue. There is, of course, no such thing as a "value-free curriculum," nor is it likely that the curricula that include community service are designed to enlist "impressionable youths for causes dear to the hearts of graying activists." In making such an assumption, the authors imply that young people are, in effect, a kind of tabula rasa, although many of these same young people are exposed daily to the problems of poverty, unsafe streets, family disruption, and deterioration of the environment.

Service Learning in Early Adolescence

Melinda Fine, in her book *Habits of Mind: Struggling over Values in America's Classrooms*, explores antiracism and moral education curricula in their political context. She details her observations of a seventh-grade classroom where one such curriculum, "Facing History and Ourselves," was the focus of the social studies class for one semester and concludes "that young people are ready and eager to reckon with conflicting differences in American society, and that schools must prepare them to do so responsibly" (Fine, 1995, xiii).

Service learning, when thoughtfully planned and implemented, is a powerful medium for conveying the attitudes and behaviors of responsible citizenship. It is particularly appropriate in the middle grades and high school. As they advance in school, and as their own worlds expand, students' questions and concerns embrace issues of social justice, inequities of opportunity and resources, racial harmony and intergroup conflict—in short, the issues that responsible citizenship requires us all, young and old, to confront.

These concerns can seem overwhelming even to adults with years of experience in social action and community development. The feelings of inadequacy that are often one aspect of early adolescence may be intensified as the awareness of unsolved societal problems grows. Service learning and community involvement can counteract that sense of helplessness, empowering young people to address some of these problems on a local level. Teenagers will not create world peace, nor will hunger and poverty vanish as a result of their efforts. But lonely residents of a nursing home may see the world as a friendlier place when a group of 12-year-olds visits regularly; a vacant lot, filled with trash, may become a playground, making an unsafe neighborhood safer for its children; young mediators, trained in conflict resolution, may help their peers to resolve their differences peacefully.

A service-learning approach that is well suited to the preadolescent and adolescent years allows young people to explore their community, to identify community needs, and to propose ways to meet those needs. In so doing, they also learn about themselves and others—their strengths and weaknesses, their interests, qualities of leadership, and more. They develop a plan of action and experience the effectiveness of thoughtful group effort. Their budding altruism and their indignation over perceived injustice find an outlet in positive action.

But the early teens are also the years when, as any parent or teacher of young adolescents will attest, youngsters are often restless, even volatile; their moods and attention fluctuate unpredictably; a seventh- or eighth-grade classroom, for example, often gives the impression of constant motion—feet shuffle, papers flutter to the floor, pencils role across desktops. It is what one middle school principal describes as "the age of twitch." The hands-on opportunities associated with service learning allow for the active participation and change of pace that can provide an outlet for this restlessness, while variations in classroom process and activity engage their interest and energy.

Projects of community improvement offer other benefits. It is not uncommon for adults to characterize teenagers as uncaring, out of control, or worse; these stereotypes are dispelled as teens become visible as contributors to the community. In turn, the young people who have experienced the community as unwelcoming begin to develop a sense of belonging when they create even small-scale positive change. John Kretzman and Paul Schmitz, in an essay titled "It Takes a Child to Raise a Whole Village," suggest that the adage their title reverses "is incomplete at best." They continue:

> In the cliché, . . . young folks are the objects of the action, never the subjects. They are passive and useless. They are defined as deficient—of knowledge, of skills, of any useful capacities—and relegated with their cohorts to the filling stations we call schools. The assumption is that, magically, at age 18 or 21, they will emerge . . . and re-enter the community as full and useful contributors. Clearly, as individuals and as communities, we need to re-examine how we view young people and their role in our society. . . . Whether "A" students or drop-outs, all-star athletes or suburban skateboarders, young people can help raise our villages when they are seen as individuals and capacities, with ideas and enthusiasm. (Kretzman and Schmitz, 1995, 8)

Early adolescence, as has been said, is characterized by a growing awareness of a world beyond family, neighborhood, and school, and service learning provides a way to recognize that awareness and make it a source of growth. But implicit in Kretzman and Schmitz's statement is an important message for the promoters of service learning: Engaging young people in community projects is not simply a "methodology" or an element in student learning; it is a critical component of community development. Each undertaking must stand up to the dual tests of fostering youth development and contributing to the community.

Further Components of Successful Programs

There are other important elements that the practitioner must take into account in planning for service learning in the middle grades. Checklists are seductive, but not always useful. It is tempting to list "10 qualities of successful programs of service learning," but the very nature of service learning dictates that it must be adapted to the particular needs and culture of the community in which it is embedded. There are, however, a few broad criteria, in addition to those discussed in the preceding paragraph, that apply in virtually all circumstances.

First of all, the work must be *real*. Young people are sophisticated detectors of the "phony" and will spurn "busy work." The need for their work must be apparent. The service experience is richer still when the youth have themselves identified the need and have a voice in determining the shape of the project.

Second, the project or program should constitute a good "fit" with the interests and developmental stage of the young people. Most adolescents work well with younger children. They share certain traits with preschoolers—a drive for autonomy, a need to explore and to test relationships—and perhaps this explains an affinity that seems to occur. As Sandy, a seventh-grade "helper" in the Early Adolescent Helper Program saw it, "They [the four-year-olds in the day care center] see me as part small-teacher and part big-friend." Some young people—often those whose native cultures emphasize respect for elders—relate especially well to older adults; others, unready to test themselves in interpersonal relationships, may function best in programs of environmental preservation or neighborhood improvement. By the time they reach high school, many young people are ready to take on roles as community activists. Some constraints will be imposed by the need for school-related activities to be nonpartisan, but young people have shown themselves to be effective lobbyists in curtailing hazardous waste disposal, in establishing community youth centers, and in campaigning against hunger and homelessness.

Third, the total program must be of sufficient duration, and the hands-on activity of sufficient frequency, that interpersonal relationships can develop and trust and understanding can replace diffidence or uneasiness.

Finally, regularly scheduled, ongoing reflection, with the guidance and understanding of a competent, trained adult, is crucial. Without this provision, the service becomes little more than a pleasant, "feel-good" addition to the school day. It is reflection that gives service learning lasting meaning, making it a growth experience and a precursor to continuing community involvement.

All four of these elements are basic to a successful service-learning initiative. But like most activities that seem simple, advance planning and behind-the-scenes preparation can make the difference between success and failure when service learning is introduced. The philosophical differences among educators and across the community over service learning and similar programs make it imperative to enlist in advance the support of the school administration and all community agencies that are to be involved. Equally important is the task of keeping parents and the public informed. When students are enthusiastic about a project, they can be effective communicators and may be able to assume much of this responsibility, but, in fairness, they must be able to rely on an adult advisor for guidance and backup. There are always logistical problems. Suffice it to say that taking time to anticipate and surmount these possible "glitches" in advance will allow young people and adult leaders to devote their energies to the program when it gets under way.

Many schools and youth organizations sponsor fund drives or food and clothing collections for a wide variety of nonprofit organizations. These activities, like bringing the Christmas concert to a convalescent home or preparing tray favors for a children's ward, call upon a spirit of generosity and are not without worth, but they seldom make for the transformative experience that participation in a continuing program—one that includes both hands-on activity and reflection—can become. On the other hand, there are programs of moral education or character education that depend entirely on classroom discussion; while they may emphasize character traits or behaviors that are generally seen as desirable, these curricula fail to provide the participatory experience that makes those qualities real.

> [P]roperly organized service learning projects are built around two elements. First, they involve direct experience through actual improvement projects in the community. Second, they involve reflective thought about the meaning of those experiences. . . . This blend of theory and practice, thought, and action provides the necessary ingredient to bring together the cognitive and affective dimensions which result in authentic learning. Without reflection, activities may become a random series of trial and error attempts. Without direct

experience, reflection is merely a hypothetical act lacking a test in reality. (Lipka, 1997, 59)

Experience alone, in spite of its reputation, is not "the best teacher." As Samuel Halperin points out, if it were, "we would not repeat our mistakes so often! What we do learn from is reflection on our experience" (Halperin, 1996, 35). Reflection, however, is a learned behavior, and not always easily learned. Young people—and adults—do not automatically reflect on their experiences. The setting, the presence of a knowledgeable adult leader who guides but does not control the discussion in a climate of respect for each individual's comments, will encourage participants to find meaning in their activity. Journal writing, role playing, and use of the arts to interpret activity are techniques that will help young people make sense of their experiences. The seminar or group meeting provides an opportunity to air successes and problems and to plan next steps to share what they have learned.

Group discussion—a key reflective component of service learning—contrasts with more traditional teacher-centered, content-focused classes. Even when the service-learning project is an integral part of a science or social studies class, for example, the service seminar is likely to evoke a more personal, critically reflective, and lively discussion. Because adolescence is a time of rapid change, of experiencing the world in new ways, teenagers are typically self-absorbed; when the service activity involves them in interpersonal interactions or brings them a new awareness of the many faces of injustice or misfortune, their feelings and anxieties may come to the surface in open discussion. The sensitive adult leader will find the balance that will keep the discussion constructive, will protect the participants' privacy, and will address the larger issues implicit in their service. He or she will help the young people gain new insights into both their own experiences and behaviors and the world around them. Some groups have found it useful to establish their own "ground rules" for the seminar: confidentiality is observed and respect for others—both the "clients" they serve and their fellow service providers—is emphasized. While these are important considerations, reflection also provides an opportunity for students to consider many other questions, such as, "Why is this service important in our community?" "What are the sources or causes of the circumstance we are addressing?" "Do people in other cultures have similar problems and needs? And if so, how are they addressed?"

Evaluating Service Learning

I spoke earlier of the problems in measuring the outcomes of service learning. Nevertheless, evaluation is as important in these programs as in any other area. The critical issue will be to evaluate service programs in terms of their stated goals and to guard against measuring their success in terms of goals that are not compatible with the school's philosophy. Service learning is never static—service initiatives are a response to the present and may change as the needs and climate of a community change—but the broad goals of the program will accommodate a variety of activities. If service learning is to become an accepted element in schools, there must be a clear understanding of what it can and cannot do and an honest assessment of its success in meeting the stated goals. Student participation in evaluation is particularly valuable; students gain another opportunity to serve and frequently develop information that would be difficult or impossible for an adult to elicit. Involving teachers, community organization personnel, community members, and students in addition to professional evaluators in the evaluation process will also make evaluations more credible and help to guide program improvement and modification.

Looking Ahead

Ideally, service learning should begin when children enter school, and there would be a continuum throughout the school years; a "culture of service" would be the norm. In the earliest grades, children have always had helping roles within the classroom. Just as the academic disciplines promote sequential learning, adding complexity as the learner's competence develops, participation in service and community improvement can challenge young people to increase their capacity to serve, to demonstrate caring, and to develop and act on their vision of a better society. By the time they reach high school, young people who have been steeped in this culture will be ready to propose and execute projects of their own.

If schools were indeed to become exemplars of a culture of service, the disconnect between school and "the real world" would soon diminish. Education should be a tool for integrating the diverse elements and experiences that make up the totality of a life, a way to discover how to stitch together the pieces to form a pattern. Too often we fail to appreciate the experiences children bring with them to the classroom, and so we compound the fragmentation of their lives. Service brings the community into the school, and the school into the community; the student's school experience is no longer so distinctly separated from life in the world beyond the school.

Whether the philosophical conflict between those who insist that schools "stick to the basics" and those who take an approach rooted in the work of John Dewey is seen as a struggle between left and right, or between tradition and change, it is a controversy that has yet to be resolved. Until a balance is achieved and evidence developed that academic rigor and affective education can and must be viewed as related parts of a larger whole, the culture of service will remain only a vision in most schools.

Notes

1. For descriptions of classroom activities connecting service-learning activities and specific disciplines at the middle school level, *see Teaching and Learning: Helpers' Service across the Curriculum*, available from the National Helpers Network, New York, N.Y.

References

Blyth, D., and P. Scales. 1997. Third generation of service-learning research yields more thorough data. *The Generator*, Winter.

Fine, M. 1995. *Habits of mind: Struggling over values in America's classrooms.* San Francisco: Jossey-Bass.

Finn, C., and G. Vanourek. 1995. Charity begins at school. *Commentary,* 100(4).

Gardner, J. 1992. *Reinventing community.* A Carnegie Corporation occasional paper. New York: Carnegie Corporation.

Goodlad, J. 1997. On shifting reform debate from utility to humanity. *Education Week,* 27(3), 37.

Halperin, S. 1996. Academics and life. *Education Week,* May 1.

Howe, H. 1972. *Openness—The new kick in education.* A Ford Foundation Reprint. New York: The Ford Foundation.

Kraft, R. 1996. Service learning: An introduction to its theory, practice, and effects. *Education and Urban Society,* 29(2), February.

Kretzman, J., and P. Schmitz. 1995. It takes a child to raise a whole village. In *The Johnson Foundation Annual Report,* 1994–95. Racine, Wis.: The Johnson Foundation.

Lipka, R. 1997. Research and evaluation in service learning: What do we need to know? In J. Schine (Ed.), *Service learning: 96th yearbook of the National Society for the Study of Education, Part I.* Chicago: University of Chicago Press.

Nathan, J. 1990. Toward a vision of students as "citizens." *Education Week,* April 25.

National Commission on Excellence in Education. 1983. *A nation at risk: The imperative for educational reform.* Washington, D.C.: USDE.

Rifkin, J. 1996. An interview with Jeremy Rifkin: The information age and the civil society. *Phi Delta Kappan,* 77(9).

Schaps, E., V. Battistich, and R. Solomon. 1987. School as a caring community: A key to character education. In A. Molnar (Ed.), *The construction of children's character: 96th yearbook of the National Society for the Study of Education, Part II.* Chicago: University of Chicago Press.

Chapter 3

In the Service of What?
The Politics of Service Learning

Joseph Kahne and Joel Westheimer

In his inaugural address, President John F. Kennedy challenged the nation with this famous appeal: "Ask not what your country can do for you, ask what you can do for your country." Two decades later, in a campaign speech, Ronald Reagan asked, "Are you better off today than you were four years ago?" If Kennedy's exhortation reflected the idealism and sense of collective mission that characterized the tumultuous 1960s, Reagan's question epitomized the individualism and materialism of the 1980s. In the 1990s, however, a glimmer of Kennedy's notion of service to the community and the nation is re-emerging in schools in the form of service learning.

Educators and legislators alike maintain that service learning can improve the community and invigorate the classroom, providing rich educational experiences for students at all levels of schooling. Service learning makes students active participants in service projects that aim to respond to the needs of the community while furthering the academic goals of students. Students in a service-learning project might analyze and monitor the composition of nearby swamplands or produce an oral history of their community. They might work with the homeless or initiate a cross-age tutoring project. In addition to helping those whom they serve, service-learning activities are intended to promote students' self-esteem, to develop higher-order thinking skills, to make use of multiple abilities, and to provide authentic learning experiences—all goals of current curriculum reform efforts.

Recognizing the potential of service learning, policy makers, legislators, and educators have promoted initiatives at the local, state, and national levels. The National and Community Service Act of 1990 and President Clinton's National Service Trust Act of 1993 are some recent and far-reaching examples of this trend. Millions of dollars are targeted for educators around the country, and many service-learning programs are supported by city- and statewide initiatives.[1]

As is commonly the case with new policy initiatives, however, more attention has been focused on moving forward than on asking where we are headed. While service learning advocates rush to forge coalitions and find a shared vocabulary that accommodates multiple agendas, and while practitioners and researchers begin to work on difficult implementation and evaluation issues, educators from schoolhouse to university to statehouse are neglecting to answer the most fundamental question: In the service of what?

Proponents of service learning have worked to find common ground among Democrats and Republicans, conservatives and liberals, business leaders and community activists. Edward Kennedy, Bill Clinton, George Bush, William F. Buckley, and Ralph Nader have all gone on record as strong advocates of service learning in American schools. Yet controversial issues surrounding the means and ends of service learning have been pushed to the background.

What values do service-learning curricula model and seek to promote? What kind of social and political relations do they ask students to imagine? What kinds of relationships develop between students and those they serve? What kind of society is it that service-learning students work to achieve? With the current interest in and allocation of resources to service learning comes a growing need to clarify the ideological perspectives that underlie service-learning programs.

Drawing on our year-long study of two dozen K–12 teachers who took part in a university-based effort to promote service learning in area schools, we propose a conceptual scheme that highlights different rationales for service learning. Our goal is not to replace consensus with conflict but rather to point out the various ideological, political, and social goals that can be promoted through service-learning activities in schools. We begin with two examples from our study.[2]

Two Service-Learning Cases

Consider "Serving Those in Need," Mr. Johnson's project for his twelfth-grade U.S. government course. As the class studied issues surrounding democracy and citizenship, Mr. Johnson had his students participate in community service projects of their own choosing. For example, one student worked in a center for babies whose mothers had high levels of crack cocaine in their bloodstreams during pregnancy. Another worked in a hospital, running errands for doctors and helping patients locate the sites of their appointments. A third student prepared and distributed survival kits for the homeless. By finding and engaging in community service activities, Mr. Johnson explained, students would interact with those less fortunate than themselves and experience the excitement and joy of learning while using the community as a classroom.

Ms. Adams, a seventh-grade teacher at Lexington Middle School, took a different approach. Ms. Adams and her students together identified issues of common concern and then voted to focus on the issue of homelessness. Their service-learning unit "Homelessness Here and Elsewhere" examined the social, economic, legal, and political determinants of homelessness around the world and in the local community. The class invited speakers from homeless advocacy groups, created files of newspaper articles on homelessness, and read, among other items, *No Place to Be: Voices of Homeless Children* (Berck, 1992). They developed action plans to aid relief efforts for the homeless in their own communities and raised funds for two homeless advocacy groups that the class had selected. During whole-class and small-group discussions and also in writing, they reflected on the readings, on what they had learned from the invited speakers, and on their experiences while working on the project.

These two service-learning projects have much in common. Both provide authentic learning experiences, reflection on matters of social concern, and opportunities for interdisciplinary study linked to curricular goals. Moreover, the goals of both projects have broad-based appeal. They stress the importance of compassion for those in need, and they encourage children and young adults to find ways to help.

But what of the differences? The approach to service learning taken by Mr. Johnson stresses charity and the ways in which participating in service and reflection can develop students' sense of altruism. Mr. Johnson's students gave their time and energy to help individuals and groups in need, either directly (e.g., the student who helped patients in a hospital find their appointment locales) or indirectly (e.g., preparing survival kits for the homeless). Mr. Johnson's curriculum included only minimal attention to any systematic analysis of the ills his students were helping to alleviate. Instead, his class focused on inculcating a sense of civic duty. His high school seniors were not asked to articulate an understanding of the conditions and contexts that might have contributed to the loss of a family's income or to a pregnant mother's decision to turn to crack cocaine.

Ms. Adams's students, by contrast, began their work with a systematic and critical analysis of the causes of homelessness and of the strategies employed to prevent it. The class discussed the growing economic disparity between rich and poor, the impact of homelessness on children, and the difficult balance between individual rights and collective responsibility. Students read stories by homeless children and wrote essays assessing the impact of homelessness on people like themselves.

These two orientations (and they are by no means neatly distinct from one another) have a long history in debates over curriculum. The "project method" and related approaches often include a service component that emphasizes change. For past reformers, such as John Dewey, William Kilpatrick, George Counts, and Paul Hanna, the transformative potential of this approach was of prime importance. These curriculum theorists and educational reformers wanted students to engage in service-learning projects so they would recognize that their academic abilities and collective commitments could help them respond in meaningful ways to a variety of social concerns.[3]

For Dewey, this ideal was the essence of democratic education. He argued for the creation of "miniature communities" in which students would work together to identify and respond to problems they confronted. The value of this approach extended far beyond the service students might provide for the elderly or the ways they might clean up the environment. It lay in the analytic and academic skills, the moral acuity, and the social sensitivity students would develop as they learned to assess critically and respond collectively to authentic problems. The hope was that students' values and beliefs might be transformed by these experiences. As Lawrence Cremin explains, these educators believed that "by manipulating the school curriculum, they could ultimately change the world" (1988, 187). Thus, *Dare the Schools Build a New Social Order?* was the aptly chosen title of George Counts's widely read book.

In contrast, much of the current discussion of service learning emphasizes charity, not change. The claim regarding the relation of service learning to the development of altruism is relatively simple to articulate and, in many respects, compelling. By engaging in meaningful service—whether tutoring children for whom English is a second language, helping patients in a hospital, doing difficult chores for the elderly, or supervising younger children's recreational activities—students will have opportunities to experience what David Hornbeck, former Maryland state superintendent, referred to as "the joy of reaching out to others" (1987, 2). For example, many students left Mr. Johnson's project aware of the contributions they could make toward helping others and eager to continue the work they began as part of the course.

The argument for the development of altruism was also advanced by Ernest Boyer of the Carnegie Foundation for the Advancement of Teaching. Boyer wrote that "altruism can best be appreciated as an experience rather than an abstraction." He endeavored to create "a new Carnegie unit," the requirement that all students take part in volunteer activities in their school or community as a condition for graduation from high school (Boyer, 1987, ix).

The Moral, Political, and Intellectual Domains

Just as the difference between change and charity may provide an important conceptual distinction for those analyzing service-learning curricula, it is helpful to distinguish the moral, political, and intellectual goals that motivate those who support service learning. These goals are summarized in table 1.

In the moral domain, service-learning activities tend toward two types of relationships. Those relationships which emphasize charity we will call "giving." Those which aim primarily to deepen relationships and to forge new connections we will call "caring." In caring relationships, Nel Noddings asserts, we try to consider the life and disposition of those for whom we are caring. We attempt to "apprehend the reality of the other" and then to "struggle [for progress] together" (1984, 14–15). In so doing, we create opportunities for changing our understanding of the other and the context within which he or she lives.

Table 1   Service-Learning Goals

	Moral	**Political**	**Intellectual**
Charity	Giving	Civic duty	Additive experience
Change	Caring	Social reconstruction	Transformative experience

In the political domain, the intentions of those promoting service-learning activities draw from two different assumptions about political socialization and what it means to be a citizen. Those who focus primarily on charity believe that to be properly educated in a democracy, students must undergo experiences that demonstrate the value of altruism and the dangers of exclusive self-interest. They stress the importance of civic duty and the need for responsive citizens. Volunteerism and compassion for the less fortunate are the undergirding conceptions of political socialization associated with this vision.

The second notion of political socialization reveals fundamentally different assumptions about the requirements of citizenship. Those promoting this vision of service learning hope to move students toward participation in what Benjamin Barber (1984) refers to as a "strong democracy." They call for a curriculum that emphasizes critical reflection about social policies and conditions, the acquisition of skills of political participation, and the formation of social bonds.

In the intellectual domain, a service-learning curriculum can further a number of goals. The ability of a service-learning curriculum to foster authentic, experience-based learning opportunities, to motivate students, to help students engage in higher-order thinking in contextually varied environments, and to promote interdisciplinary studies has led some, such as John Brisco, a leader in the field, to label service learning "the Trojan horse of school reform." The service component may help us get the support needed for implementation, he argues, but the real impact of service learning has to do with its ability to promote powerful learning environments.

Educators who emphasize change would clearly also value the educational benefits of this approach. To tap into the full power of service activities, however, these practitioners would want to combine critical inquiry with action. This process can transform students' understandings of both disciplinary knowledge and the particular social issues with which they are engaged.

The Challenge for Practitioners and Advocates

We do not mean to imply that the contents of table 1 represent discrete categories. As we will show, the underlying goals and the impact of a given service-learning activity can embody commitments to both change and charity and can have relevance for any of the three domains. Indeed, these domains are not discrete; moral, political, and intellectual goals are intertwined. Moreover, the same activities may be experienced quite differently by different students. Finally, this framework is not exhaustive. Service learning can advance other priorities, such as the acquisition of vocational skills.

To note the limits of these distinctions, however, is not to deny their value. These categories can help clarify our understanding of the possible relationships shared by service-learning activities, their outcomes, and the goals that motivate their design.

Moral Domain: Giving and Caring

As was true during the Progressive era, many who currently advocate service learning consider its potential as a means of promoting moral development.[4] In many service-learning projects the emphasis is on giving and on countering the narcissism that is believed to be so prevalent among young people and in the society generally. The idea that educators should foster a volunteer ethic and encourage youths to give something back to their school or community currently receives widespread support. It is voiced by educators and politicians alike.[5] Sen. Edward Kennedy (D-Mass.) points out, for example, that "90% of 14- to 17-year-olds who had been asked to volunteer [for public service] did so" (1991, 772). And President Bush made famous the image of "a thousand points of light," representing the innumerable efforts of citizens to respond to America's social problems.

One student in Mr. Johnson's class, for example, volunteered at the Veterans' Memorial Senior Center: "For Thanksgiving this year my stepmother and I helped serve the seniors their Thanksgiving dinner. This was a very rewarding experience helping others in need. It seemed that the dinner was something special to them, it was a chance for them to get together with their peers. Many don't have families in the area and are all alone for the holidays. This made it a little less lonely, which feels great. Thank you for giving me the chance to help!"

This experience and others like it, quite common in the service literature, emphasize charity more than change. The experience was structured to promote giving rather than to provide the kind of understanding needed for the development of caring relationships. As a result, the student's description of the event lacked the perspective and input of those she was helping.

Similarly, the student in Mr. Johnson's class who assembled "daily life kits," which he then distributed to the homeless in San Francisco, determined the kits' contents without ever talking with homeless individuals or with those who had knowledge on the subject.[6] He experienced the joys of service, but he had few opportunities for meaningful interactions through which caring relationships and understanding might develop. When I care, Noddings explains, a relationship develops in which "the other's reality becomes a real possibility for me" (1984, 14). The distance between the one caring and one cared for diminishes. Unfortunately, in many service activities, students view the people they serve as clients rather than as a resource.

However, there are numerous ways in which curriculum focused on giving provides opportunities for students to develop caring relationships, especially when compared with a traditional academic curriculum. For example, a music director at a middle school we studied wanted her suburban, upper-middle-class students to perform at a nearby elementary school in a poor neighborhood. Some of the middle school parents objected, saying that they were concerned for their children's safety. In a written evaluation, the students said that they had imagined "horrifying children running around on a dirty campus." They had expected them to be "rude, tough, noisy and very unfriendly," and they even thought they would be "mean, gang-related blacks." One of the students wrote, "I was scared because my mom had told me it was a bad neighborhood and to be careful."

After they returned, students' perspectives on the elementary school children had changed. They were "surprised at the children's responsiveness and their attentiveness," they found the children to be "extremely polite and surprisingly friendly," and they discovered that they "listened well and had excellent behavior." One student wrote, "Everyone at the school had good manners, and I think more highly of [the neighborhood] now." The experiential and interpersonal components of service-learning activities can help students take the first crucial step toward diminishing the sense of "otherness" that often separates students—particularly privileged students—from those in need. In so doing, the potential to develop caring relationships is created.

Political Domain: Responsible Citizens
and Critical Democrats

Rather than tie the service curriculum exclusively to moral development, some advocates of service learning talk about developing citizens for our democracy. While there is widespread commitment to this goal,[7] there are important differences in what people mean by "developing citizens." Merging the rhetoric of altruism with notions of citizenship, some argue that good citizens should perform community service as a kind of charity. Many agree with Sen. Kennedy, who writes that democracy "means . . . the responsibility to give something back to America in return for all it has given us" (1991, 772). Similarly, the chief rationale for the community service requirement in Atlanta was that it would make students recognize "the responsibility of good citizens to help others" (Harrison, 1987, 11). Mr. Johnson, who shares this logic, explains to his students and their parents that he makes "community service . . . a vital part of the government course [because] part of citizenship is the practice of helping others in the community."

Others argue that educators may miss important opportunities if they disconnect the act of service from critical examination of the setting in which it occurs. While requiring students to "serve America" (the rhetoric of the federal legislation) might produce George Bush's "thousand points of light," it might also promote a thousand points of the status quo. Indeed, the emphasis on altruism and charity, so common in many recent service-learning initiatives, is often used to back a conservative political agenda that denies a role for government. Note George Bush's rhetoric as he voiced his support for the National Community Services Act of 1990: "I am particularly pleased that [this act] will promote an ethic of community service. . . . Government cannot rebuild a family or reclaim a sense of neighborhood, and no bureaucratic program will ever solve the pressing human problems that can be addressed by a vast galaxy of people working voluntarily in their own backyards" (quoted in Radest, 1993, 8).

Bush was advancing voluntary community service as an alternative to government programs. He made no mention of changes that address the structural injustices that leave so many in need. This kind of service runs the risk of being understood as a kind of noblesse oblige— a private act of kindness performed by the privileged. This distinction is hardly a new one. Paul Hanna, in his 1937 book, *Youth Serves the Community*, criticized efforts to serve that provided token amounts of needed aid yet never identified or responded to structural problems. "Time and energy given to such superficial betterment [Hanna gives as an example making Thanksgiving baskets for poor families] could much more efficiently be spent in getting at the basic inhibiting influences which perpetuate a scarcity economy in the midst of abundance" (1937, 40).

Similarly, many contemporary scholars focus on change over charity and argue that the lack of connection between individual rights and communal obligations within our culture has left us with a bankrupt sense of citizenship. Like the programs Hanna criticized more than 50 years ago, many current service activities emphasize altruism and charity and fail to call into question current notions of individualism or to encourage the type of political participation that furthers democracy. "Democratic politics," Benjamin Barber writes, "has become something we watch rather than something we do" (1984, 235). Our participation in acts of national service, he believes, is a "prerequisite of citizenship" and essential for democratic institutions: "The thousand points of light through which the lucky serve the needy may help illuminate our humanity, but they cannot warm or nurture our common soul, nor create a sense of common responsibility connected to our liberty, nor provide integral solutions to structural problems. The model is compassion or charity; [service is optional, a personal choice] and thus can never be the subject of political duties" (Barber, 1984, 235).

This, then, is a fundamental critique of those who market the importance of service learning by referencing both the motivation and joy that come from giving and the importance of altruism. Barber would disagree with Diane Hedin when she writes, "Maybe this [community service] is what citizenship is all about, acting in a decent way toward people who live where we live" (quoted in Harrison, 1987, 5). Citizenship in a democratic community requires more than kindness and decency; it requires engagement in complex social and institutional endeavors. Acts of civic duty cannot replace government programs or forms of collective social action. Citizenship requires that individuals work to create, evaluate, criticize, and change public institutions and programs.

And such action is unavoidably political. Thus, Harry Boyte is critical of current conceptions of service because they meet students' needs for "personal relevance and a sense of membership in a community. [But] volunteers usually disavow concern with larger policy questions, seeing service as an *alternative* to politics" (emphasis in original; Boyte, 1991, 776). This attitude is reflected in the words of a university undergraduate, which were included in the William T. Grant Foundation's influential report *The Forgotten Half*:

> Students tutor, coach softball, paint playgrounds, and read to the elderly because they are interested in people, or because they want to learn a little about poverty and racism before they head out into the waiting corporate world. . . . We do not volunteer "to make a statement," or to use the people we work with to protest something. We try to see the homeless man, the

hungry child, and the dying woman as the people they are, not the means to some political end. (Commission on Work, Family, and Citizenship, 1988, 81)

By contrast, those oriented toward change embrace the importance of political activity. Boyte, for example, believes that service activities should develop students' abilities at "public speaking, recruiting other students, organizing meetings, analyzing problems, developing action plans, and conducting evaluations" (1991, 767).

The curriculum developed by Katharine Isaac (1992), titled *Civics for Democracy: A Journey for Teachers and Students*, illustrates some of what this approach might imply for today's high school students.[8] The first section focuses on profiles of students in action. It describes the efforts of high school students in Florida to limit deforestation in the southern part of their state; an effort by students in Fargo, North Dakota, to boycott the institutionalization of Whittle Communications' Channel One; and a variety of other efforts by which students gained a sense of what activism can accomplish. The curriculum also includes opportunities to study the history of various citizen movements (civil rights movement, labor movement, women's rights movement, consumer movement, environmental movement). Students examine both the substantive themes of these movements and the strategies that actors with diverse agendas employed. Numerous ideas for change-oriented student projects that include research and action are also explored. These projects range from evaluating the representativeness of juries to analyzing the evening news to improving the availability of child care. This curriculum highlights the explicitly political nature of service and community action, teaches meaningful skills in a systematic manner, and integrates these ideas with academic investigations.

Intellectual Domain: Additive and Transformative
Given the educational focus of service-learning activities, no analysis would be complete without considering the activities from the perspective of intellectual development. Service-learning advocates agree that experiential, active pedagogy is often quite powerful. While an additional emphasis on charity might lead to service-learning activities that raise self-esteem, impel students into new experiences, and demonstrate the value of scholastic abilities in real-world contexts, educators who focus on a transformative vision would want to carry this work one step further. For them, it is the combination of service and

critical analysis, not either by itself, that is most likely to promote interest in and insight into these complex social issues.

Of course, neither of these outcomes is assured. Indeed, there is reason for concern that service experiences frequently fail to achieve either additive or transformative goals. Consider again Mr. Johnson's service curriculum in which each student designed his or her own project. By providing materials and access to knowledgeable speakers, Mr. Johnson prompted his students to consider various projects, but the students ultimately had to make their own arrangements. The focus and quality of the projects they developed varied enormously. Some students became an integral part of an organization; others performed busy work. One student's project was to do chores around the house for her grandmother. Some students spoke of new insights; others did not. There was no meaningful reflective component to this project. It required simply that students submit a one- or two-paragraph summary of their efforts. Their grade depended primarily on the number of hours they volunteered. Thirty hours for an A, 20 for a B, 10 for a C.

The example of Mr. Johnson's service curriculum is particularly relevant, because its design mirrors large-scale initiatives to promote community service around the country. For example, students in Atlanta must complete 75 hours of volunteer service to graduate. Maryland now requires that all high school students perform 75 hours of community service prior to graduation or participate in an alternative district program approved by the state. There are also major efforts in Vermont, New York, the District of Columbia, Pennsylvania, and Minnesota, and the number of initiatives around the nation is growing. Some of these proposals work to integrate reflection on the service activities; others do not. In Atlanta students simply write a 500-word essay describing their experiences. They never discuss their experiences as part of a course. In fact, many of the major legislative proposals have a minimal reflective component, sometimes for fear that such an orientation would diminish the focus on altruism.

The importance of a meaningful reflective component becomes clearer when one considers the kind of deliberation and student empowerment that such a curriculum can foster. Recall the service project in which middle school music students from an affluent community performed for and met with elementary school students in a nearby poor community. This interaction led some students to report marked changes in their beliefs about children from this neighborhood. Moreover, when asked what they gained from the experience, many students said simply that it taught them "that people can be different" from what you expect. Others arrived at a variety of deeper insights: "[The neighborhood] isn't as bad as the news makes it out to be." "The rumors I have heard are a big bunch of hogwash. . . . I'm glad I went on that trip because it was a wonderful experience to meet new people and find out about their lives." These statements testify to the transformative power of service-learning experiences. The effect could become even greater if students discussed the possible causes of these rumors and their impact.

Almost all discussions of service-learning practices emphasize the importance of reflection.[9] For the most part, however, descriptions of reflective activities do not include the kind of critical analysis that might help students step outside dominant understandings to find new solutions. Clearly, having students share their thoughts and experiences with one another can be valuable, but reflective activities (commonly in the form of journal entries and discussions) may only reinforce previously held beliefs and simplistic, if generous, conclusions.[10] Moreover, as Richard Paul makes clear, students may use their developing ability to articulate powerful logical arguments to "maintain their most deep-seated prejudices and irrational habits of thought by making them appear more rational" (1990, 370).

A transformative educational experience, on the other hand, requires that students engage in critical thinking in the "strong" rather than "weak" sense. To be critical thinkers, students must be able to consider arguments that justify conclusions that conflict with their own predispositions and self-interest.[11] Structured, informed, and systematic analysis of service experiences from a variety of ideological positions will not ensure critical thinking in the strong sense, but such reflection should make that outcome more common.

Service Is Political

Efforts to integrate service-learning activities into the curriculum have great potential and deserve the support they are now receiving. To date, however, little attention has been given to sorting out the goals and motivations that underlie the spectrum of service-learning projects emerging in schools throughout the country. Is it beneficial to point out such differences and risk creating some opposition to service learning? We think so. Clarifying different goals provides educators with an opportunity to consider systematically a range of possible priorities (including some they might otherwise not consider) and the relation of these to their practice.

Moreover, it is important to acknowledge that the choice of service-learning activities—like the choice of any curricular activity—has political dimensions. Currently, the most broadly supported (and therefore most politically tenable) goal for service-learning activities is to convey to students the importance of charity. If we were to focus on the "numerous values we share as a community," writes Amitai Etzioni, the founder of the communitarian movement and a proponent of service learning, "our world would be radically improved" (1993, 97). While such rhetoric might allow this political scientist to be a trusted adviser to members of Congress on both sides of the aisle, it will not resolve the dilemmas facing practitioners who need to think carefully about the many values that we do *not* share, about what a radically improved world might look like, and about the different ways one might pursue this goal.

Rather than assume, erroneously, that all educators share the same vision, we think it is better to be explicit about the numerous and different visions that drive the creation and implementation of service-learning activities in schools. "In the service of what?" is a question that inevitably merits the attention of teachers, policy makers, and academicians who take seriously the idea that learning and service reinforce each other and should come together in America's schools.

Acknowledgments

The authors would like to thank Bill Ayers, Barbara Leckie, Rebekah Levin, Denise Pope-Clark, Gordon Pradl, John Rogers, Bill Schubert, Steve Tozer, and Jim Youniss for their feedback.

Notes

1. Major initiatives with links to graduation requirements are under way in Atlanta, New York, Maryland, Vermont, Pennsylvania, the District of Columbia, and numerous other districts throughout the country.

2. We draw on data from interviews and surveys of teachers and students, from classroom observations, and from project reports submitted by the teachers. We would like to thank all those who participated in the service-learning minigrants program, but the names of teachers and schools discussed here have been changed.

3. See, for example, Dewey, 1916, 1956; Kilpatrick, 1918; Counts, 1932; and Hanna, 1936.

4. For the Progressive era, see Dewey, 1909, and Hanna, 1936. For contemporaries, see Cognetta and Sprinthall, 1978, and Etzioni, 1993.

5. For the voices of educators, see Boyer, 1987; Conrad and Hedin, 1991; and Nathan and Kielsmeier, 1991.

6. The kits included items for personal grooming (a comb, a razor, a toothbrush, toothpaste, soap, and shampoo) and a small Bible.

7. See Kennedy, 1991; Boyer, 1987; Barber, 1992; and Isaac, 1992.

8. See also Newmann, 1974.

9. For a fine example, see Honnet and Poulsen, 1989.

10. For example, the Council of Chief State School Officers' report on service learning states that a service-learning curriculum "should provide for a structured period for reflection after the service experience, when the students can think, talk, and/or write about what they saw and did" (Council of Chief State School Officers, 1989, 5). It does not mention the need to consider these experiences in relation to systematic academic work.

11. See Paul, 1990, 373.

References

Barber, B. 1984. *Strong democracy: Participatory politics for a new age.* Berkeley: University of California Press.

———. 1992. *An aristocracy for everyone.* New York: Ballantine Books.

Berck, J. 1992. *No place to be: Voices of homeless children.* Boston: Houghton Mifflin.

Boyer, E. 1987. Foreword. In C. Harrison, *Student service: The new Carnegie unit.* New Jersey: The Carnegie Foundation for the Advancement of Teaching.

Boyte, H. 1991. Community service and civic education. *Phi Delta Kappan,* 72: 765–767.

Cognetta, P., and N. Sprinthall. 1978. Students as teachers: Role taking as a means of promoting psychological and ethical development during adolescence. In N. Sprinthall and R. Mosher (Eds.), *Value development as the aim of education.* Schenectady, N.Y.: Character Research Press.

Commission on Work, Family, and Citizenship, 1988. *The forgotten half: Pathways to success for America's youth and young families.* Washington, D.C.: William T. Grant Foundation.

Conrad, D., and D. Hedin. 1991. School-based community service: What we know from research and theory. *Phi Delta Kappan,* 72: 743–749.

Council of Chief State School Officers, 1989. *Community service learning by doing.* Washington, D.C.: Council of Chief State School Officers.

Counts, G. 1932. *Dare the schools build a new social order?* New York: John Day.

Cremin, L. 1988. *American education: The metropolitan experience, 1876–1980.* New York: Harper and Row.

Dewey, J. 1909. *Moral principles in education.* In J. Boydston (Ed.), *The middle works: 1899–1924.* Carbondale: Southern Illinois University Press.

———. J. 1916. *Schools of tomorrow,* New York: E. P. Dutton and Company.

———. 1956. *The school and society.* In J. Dewey, *The Child and the curriculum and the school and society.* Chicago: University of Chicago Press.

Etzioni, A. 1993. *The spirit of community: Rights, responsibilities, and the communitarian agenda.* New York: Crown Publishers.

Hanna, P. 1936. *Youth serves the community.* New York: D. Appleton Century.

Harrison, C. 1987. *Student service: The new Carnegie unit.* New Jersey: The Carnegie Foundation for the Advancement of Teaching.

Honnet, E., and S. Poulsen. 1989. *Principles of good practice for combining service and learning: Wingspread special report.* Racine, Wis.: Johnson Foundation.

Isaac, K. 1992. *Civics for democracy: A journey for teachers and students.* A Project of the Center for Study of Responsive Law and Essential Information. Washington, D.C.: Essential Books.

Kennedy, E. 1991. National service and education for citizenship. *Phi Delta Kappan,* 72: 771–773.

Kilpatrick, W. 1918. The project method. *Teachers College Record,* September, 319–35.

Nathan, J., and J. Kielsmeier. 1991. The sleeping giant of school reform. *Phi Delta Kappan,* 72: 739–742.

Newmann, F. 1974. *Education for citizen action: Challenge for secondary curriculum.* Berkeley, Calif.: McCutchan.

Noddings, N. 1984. *Caring: A feminine approach to ethics and moral education.* Berkeley: University of California Press.

Paul, R. 1990. *Critical thinking: What every person needs to survive in a rapidly changing world.* Rohnert Park, Calif.: Center for Critical Thinking and Moral Critique.

Radest, H. 1993. *Community service: Encounter with strangers.* Westport, Conn.: Praeger.

Chapter 4

Promoting Identity Development: Ten Ideas for School-Based Service-Learning Programs

Miranda Yates and James Youniss

After working four times at a soup kitchen as part of a year-long service learning program, a 16-year-old high school junior summarized her experiences in this way: "Going to the soup kitchen made me realize how extreme the problem is. How it affected many races and people of all ages. I knew this problem existed, but it didn't have a face until I went to the soup kitchen. Talking with people made me want to work harder to do something more besides serve soup." This quotation illustrates that working at a soup kitchen can encourage participants to think about their relationship to other people in new ways. This student expresses not only an increased sense of personal connection to people who are homeless but also a burgeoning commitment to confront social problems. Serving at the soup kitchen encouraged her to reflect on issues pertinent to moral awareness and self-understanding. Moreover, she ties these issues together by connecting her change in understanding of other people to thinking about what she wants to do in the future. This type of reflection suggests that service learning can influence adolescents' sense of identity *and* social justice.

This chapter explores the relationship between school-based service-learning programs and identity development in adolescence. We present a theoretical perspective that connects service-learning experience to identity development and outline the programmatic implications of this perspective. In the first part of the chapter, we describe current efforts to promote school-based service programs and criticisms of these efforts. We proceed to argue that service has the potential to be an identity-defining experience that heightens societal connectedness and social responsibility. The second part of this chapter applies our theoretical perspective to the implementation of programs. We identify 10 ideas for promoting identity development. Data from a mandatory school-based program help us to illustrate these ideas.

Current Debate on School-Based Service-Learning Programs

In the 1990s, school-based service learning has been promoted by federal, state, and local funding and legislation as well as by corporate projects and media coverage. Currently, the federally funded Corporation for National and Community Service apportions part of its grants to school-based programs via its Learn-and-Serve program. It also finances the National Service-Learning Cooperative/Clearinghouse, which disseminates information on implementing programs. On a state and local level, a recent survey of the 130 largest school districts in the United States estimated that 15% require service district wide and 44% have at least one school requiring service (National and Community Service Coalition, 1995). Exemplifying corporate interest, the Prudential Insurance Company of America commissioned a national survey of youth volunteerism (Wirthlin Group, 1996) and began the Spirit of Community Awards program, which recognizes the service efforts of youth in each state. Media coverage of youth service has also become quite common, and it is not unusual for newspapers to feature positively oriented stories about youth experiences in school-based programs (e.g., Smith, 1997; Strauss, 1994).

Not all media coverage of school-based service has been positive, however. The current debate about mandating service for public high school graduation has revealed differences in opinion about making service a part of school curricula. At one extreme, legal battles in North Carolina and Pennsylvania have coincided with the appearance of editorials and articles detailing objections to requiring service participation and promoting service programs (e.g., Maddox, 1996; Saunders, 1996b; Steirer, 1997). Mandated service has been criticized for infringing on the constitutional rights of students and parents and draining resources from other subjects (Bullock, 1996). Optional service programs have been denounced for promoting the decline in academic achievement in U.S. public schools (Flott, 1996).

It is notable that both advocates and critics of service-learning programs discuss this topic in terms of the character and identity of the
nation, its schools, and its student citizens. Advocates emphasize the
need to provide more opportunities for service and to reorient contemporary culture toward the value of helping others and taking up
social responsibility (Commission on National and Community Service, 1993). Many critics of service programs believe that government-
sponsored service programs smack of "Big Brother" and intrude on
individual choice and action (Saunders, 1996a). They support alter-
nate routes such as parenting for teaching the value of service (Reinhard,
1996).

On either side of the debate, discussions of service learning almost
always express concern for youth's current and future levels of civic
engagement and participation. Adolescents' understanding of how they
can be a part of and contribute to society is a central aspect of these
discussions. In this chapter, we connect this form of emerging understanding to the process of identity development and argue that service-learning programs with certain characteristics can promote societal connectedness and social responsibility.

Identity Development

The perspective on identity presented in this chapter derives from
Erikson (1968) and Inhelder and Piaget (1958). They depicted adolescence as a transitional period in contemporary Western culture and
emphasized that the capacity to engage in formal thinking combined
with societal expectations encourage adolescents to anticipate the roles
they will undertake in adulthood (Youniss and Yates, 1997). Whether
adolescents accept or reject the societal ideologies they encounter or
try to imagine future possibilities, their efforts represent a struggle to
understand their membership within a societal framework.

Erikson's (1968) prologue in *Identity: Youth and Crisis* provides a
particularly cogent account of the social-historical component of identity. He proposed that youth need ideological guides to make sense of
all that occurs around them. With these guides, youth can evaluate
and differentiate experiences and come to weigh them as more or less
worthwhile. Moreover, Erikson proposed that youth need to identify
with values that have transcendence, that supersede family and self
and have historical continuity commanding respect from others who
have lived and will live after them.

Erikson's ideas have direct applicability to the activities of service
learning. For example, student service at a soup kitchen puts adoles-

cents in touch with aspects of society that are not working well and can help develop a sense of responsibility to address social problems. This kind of experience provides fertile material for adolescents to reflect on social, moral, and political issues that transcend the immediate concerns of self and family.

Empirical research and evaluations of community service and service learning support the connection between participation and identity development. In a previously published review of 44 studies conducted over the past five decades, we found that results often pertained to one of three concepts: social relatedness, agency, or moral-political awareness (see Yates and Youniss, 1996b, for more detail). Taken together, these concepts indicate that service participation may influence identity development. *Social relatedness* focuses on service as a social activity that puts participants in contact with new people. Social opportunities associated with service participation can lead to a heightened and broadened sense of connection to other people. *Agency* refers to the idea that service provides challenges that expand participants' concept of what they are able to do and what they might do in the future. Finally, as service affects participants' connection to specific individuals that they meet and a developing sense of agency, it may also encourage new understanding about their place within a more general social framework. Studies of *moral-political awareness* relate service experience to subsequent moral and political activism and make the case that service participation in youth can influence the path taken in adulthood.

Program Implications: Ten Ideas for School-Based Programs

We now apply this theoretical approach to the development of service-learning programs. What are some of the program characteristics that promote identity development? To address this question, we describe a case study of a mandatory school-based service-learning program and offer examples of students' essay reflections, which, we argue, show them grappling with questions of identity. Based on our findings, we outline ten ideas of a school-based service-learning program. These ideas result from our efforts to integrate findings from the case study with the cumulative results from the service literature and from recommendations for high-quality service programs issued by service advocacy organizations (e.g., Alliance for Service Learning in Education Reform, 1993; Corporation for National and Community Service, 1994).

Case Study of Service-Learning Program at St. Francis High School

From 1993 to 1994, we conducted a case study of a mandatory service-learning program at St. Francis, an urban parochial high school. As part of this program, the junior class was required to serve four times (approximately 20 hours) at the same downtown soup kitchen. The students' service was part of a year-long course on social justice. An array of quantitative and qualitative data were gathered to investigate whether service participation can serve as a vehicle for engaging youth in moral and political issues as well as encouraging them to reflect on their own role in enacting change.

School and Student Characteristics

The school was located in a major northeastern city. The most frequently represented religious backgrounds were Catholic (33%) and Baptist (33%), with 7% specifying no religious background and 24% of students coming from other Christian backgrounds. In the junior class, 46% were male and 54% female. The majority (71%) were 16 years old at the beginning of the year. Individual information on ethnic and socioeconomic background was not available, but there was no reason to believe that this sample differed from the school population. According to school officials, 95% of students were black/African American, 1% white, and 4% from other ethnic backgrounds. Students came from middle- and lower-middle-class families. Information on home addresses indicated that many students came from inner-city neighborhoods marked by poverty and violence.

Table 1   Examples of Student Essay Reflections

Level 1 (Little): See a homeless person as an individual rather than as a stereotype.
"There was a man whose legs and hands were shaking. . . . What seemed to be wrong was he must be going through some type of withdrawal. . . . I finally got up the nerve to ask him what was wrong . . . he replied, 'nothing at all, but can I have me some soup?' . . . What shocked me was that I was afraid because he looked the way he looked. I was afraid of his homelessness and dirtiness. But when I took the courage to ask him what was wrong, he wasn't dirty, he became more human."

Level 2 (Intermediate): Confront consciousness of one's everyday life. Compare one's own life circumstances with another's—specifically, those of a homeless person.

"On this one trip I got to meet a variety of people I would have never seen if I was washing dishes or taking out the garbage. Even after all my encounters with the homeless I still felt these people were strange. And I continued to serve. It wasn't until one man who was passing through the line told me that the streets have messed up their heads. I thought about it and thought what would I be like if I was forced to live on the streets without knowing what the next day will bring. I go crazy when I don't have money for McDonald's. What would happen to me if I lived like they do?"

Level 3 (Bigger): Reflect on justice and responsibility. Theorize about confronting injustice through altering personal actions or societal processes.
"All of my life when I have had problems people have told me to look on the bright side. But when I look at homelessness and poverty there is no bright side. . . . If you really look at it we use the homeless and impoverished as our bright side. Whenever we have problems, whenever things don't go the way we want them to go we say look on the bright side, at least we are not homeless, at least you have food on your table. . . . Why do they have to always be our bright sides? Who's going to be their bright side? Why are we content with having a class of people below us who can make us feel better when we think of how bad they have it? Why not help them to get to where you are? Why not have a bright side come from within, rather than from people who have it bad enough as it is."

Social Justice Class

Working at the soup kitchen was a pivotal part of a year-long course on social justice required of all juniors. This course met for 50 minutes daily in six sections of 20 to 30 students. One teacher, Mr. Siwek, taught five sections and another teacher, Ms. O'Connell, taught one. All sections used the curriculum developed by Mr. Siwek over an 18-year period.

The goal of the course is well captured by one of Mr. Siwek's favorite assigned readings, a column by Jonathan Yardley. When the birthday of Martin Luther King, Jr., became a national holiday, Yardley (1986) wrote about his own college experiences advocating civil rights in a school newspaper: "It was my enormous good fortune to be at the right place at the right time: to be young, to have found a great cause, to be doing nothing of moment on its behalf, but to be doing it with all my heart." By the end of the course, teachers wanted students to be convinced that they, too, were "at the right place at the right time," that they were young and could find a great cause to fight for with all their heart. To this end, both teachers used class time to implore students to think about the moral implications of events going on around them and to care deeply about injustices. Issues discussed during the year included homelessness, poverty among families, and children, exploitation of immigrant laborers, urban violence and capital punishment, AIDS, racism, anti-Semitism, and homophobia. In addition, people such as Martin Luther King, Jr., Dorothy Day, Archbishop Oscar Romero, Cesar Chavez, and Mitch Snyder were offered as exemplars of the fight against injustice.

The course text was a compilation of articles, many from *The Washington Post, The New York Times,* and *The New Yorker.* In addition to these readings, the class viewed several films and public television programs, heard guest speakers, and participated in special events, such as reading their essays at the school food drive.

Types of Data Collected

Four types of data were collected over the 1993–1994 school year. First, questionnaires were administered during the first week of class and at the time of the final exam. Second, we made participant observations at the soup kitchen and social justice class and attended special events at the school, such as the food drive assembly, a pep rally, and the end-of-the- year assembly. Third, we ran discussion groups after each assigned trip to the soup kitchen (see Yates, 1998, for more detail on findings from the discussion groups). Fourth, student essays on the soup kitchen were collected after each assigned trip.

Essay Reflections

The students' essays illustrate how service experience encouraged them to reflect on their relationship to other people and their role in society both in the present and the future. Students used a standard one-page form to write their essays. The directions on the top of the form read: "Write a thoughtful essay about your day of service at the kitchen. Comment on the work which you did and the people you met. Did you work hard, were you needed, did you leave some love behind?" On the bottom of the form, five lines were provided to describe the "best moment of the day." While the majority of students limited their essay to one page, approximately one-third continued onto the back.

In reading over the essays, we found that about half of them went beyond descriptions of concrete events at the soup kitchen and offered reflections regarding the broader meaning of the service experience for the student's life. We coded three types of statement. At level 1 (little), students discussed seeing a homeless person as an individual rather than as a stereotype. At level 2 (intermediate), students confronted consciousness of their everyday life and compared their lot in life with that of a homeless person. Finally, at level 3 (bigger), students reflected on justice and responsibility and theorized about confronting injustice through altering personal actions or societal processes (see Yates and Youniss, 1996a, for further details about this coding scheme).

Table 1 provides examples of each level. These examples demonstrate how service experience may encourage students to examine the connections between moral and political questions and their own lives. This conclusion is strengthened by results from the focus groups, questionnaires, and observations as well as from surveys and interviews of 121 alumni who graduated three, five, and ten years earlier. We found that a large number of students wrote and talked about the service-learning program as an identity-defining experience that helped them to reflect on who they were as adolescents and who they became as adults (Youniss and Yates, 1997). In support of previous findings on the impact of service learning, students and alumni specifically described the impact of the course in terms of its influence on their sense of agency, social relatedness, and moral-political awareness. Many alumni attributed their continued involvement in community service after high school gradation to the "wake-up call to reality" they had experienced during the course.

Program Implications

What are some of the program characteristics that led this service-learning course to have such a profound positive impact on many of its students? Here, we specify 10 pivotal features, or ideas, of the course that we believe helped make it an intense experience that challenged students' preconceptions and encouraged them to feel ready and able to take on pressing societal problems.

1. The service activity is meaningful.
2. Helping others is emphasized.
3. The program is part of an articulated ideology.
4. Activities are performed as a group rather than individually.
5. Reflective opportunities with peers are provided.
6. Program organizers serve as models and integrators.
7. Site supervisors serve as models.
8. Participants' diversity is acknowledged.
9. Feeling a part of history is encouraged.
10. Acceptance of personal and social responsibility is encouraged.

These ideas may help guide decision making in designing and implementing a service-learning course. Each plays a role in encouraging those aspects of identity associated with societal relatedness and social responsibility. While we base our conclusions on a school-based program, they may have some generalizability to community-based programs as well.

1. Meaningful Activity In assessing community service programs, questions about the frequency and length of service often arise. Our case study supports the notion that quality of service is important, perhaps even more so than quantity. Students at St. Francis were required to serve at the soup kitchen for a relatively short period, on four occasions for approximately 20 hours. Yet 10 years later alumni see their experience at the kitchen as a landmark event that helped to shape who they were in high school and who they are today.

The literature on service specifies some of the qualities of a service activity that help to make it meaningful to an individual's sense of identity. In *Principles for High Quality Service Programs*, the Corporation for National and Community Service (1994) emphasizes that service activities should address real needs and consider the unique qualities, including age, of participants. Newmann and Rutter's (1983) description of "developmental opportunities" further contributes to defining meaningful service activities by identifying features such as "having responsibility to make decisions, identifying and reflecting upon one's personal values, working closely with adults, facing new and challenging situations, and receiving appropriate blame or credit for one's work done" (2).

Preparing and serving meals at a soup kitchen as part of an organized program provides these types of opportunities as do activities such as child care, hospital work, mentoring, building renovation, and park clean-up. We add to Newmann and Rutter's list one further quality of service that was central to the St. Francis students' experience and that may make some service activities more beneficial than others. In written essays and discussions groups, students focused on the profound impact of interacting with people who have been stereotyped and marginalized by society. These encounters forced many students to reflect on the conflict between their preconceptions about homeless people and the reality of individuals who urgently needed help. Often when students articulated a sense of commitment to service in the future, they framed it in terms of having been motivated by a homeless person they had met.

This motivation did not take the form of pity or charity but rather of respect for another person and moral indignation at present social conditions. For example, one student described in her final essay how an encounter with a homeless man led her to reflect on how she should respond to him:

> There was a man [at the soup kitchen]. I didn't catch his name but he had an obvious mental problem, and my classmates and I laughed at him for a few minutes. Then I realized that he was going to be like that forever. There was no one to help him and probably no one who cared. It hurt to realize that I was sitting among society's forgotten. The people I read about everyday at school and in the newspapers. I wanted to cry, but I didn't, I couldn't, they didn't need my pity. They needed my action.

The St. Francis students worked hard because they knew that their activities at the soup kitchen were not make-work. They understood that they were performing a vital service by preparing and serving a meal for people who could not afford to buy food and who were often physically ill because of the strains in their lives. They also realized that the brief exchanges and conversations they had with the people they served were an equally important part of their work. Students treated the diners with respect and, in this way, offered a form of social interaction that homeless people rarely encounter in their day-to-day lives.

The St. Francis findings support the conclusion of prior research that *meaningful activity*: (1) addresses a patent social need, (2) challenges youth to organize and take on procedural responsibilities, and (3) encourages youth to engage in social interactions with diverse people. In the St. Francis program, social interactions may have played a particularly vital role in promoting a broadened sense of social relatedness and responsibility.

2. Emphasis on Helping Others When the St. Francis students were asked to recount the "best moment of the day," they frequently focused on a moment when they had helped another individual in less fortunate circumstances. They emphasized that the diners at the kitchen really needed them and that they, in turn, cared about the diners. The act of helping others was what engaged the students. Helping included offering assistance to specific homeless individuals and soup kitchen staff as well as contributing to solve a social problem. While personal benefits such as heightened self-confidence were undoubtedly derived, emphasis was placed on the other more than on the self.

This finding bears on Kahne and Westheimer's (1996) analysis of the "politics" of renewed interest in community service in the 1980s and 1990s. They voice concern that much of the rhetoric advocating service is presented within the framework of charity and places inordinate emphasis on personal benefits to the participating youth. They find fault with such goals and especially single out the goal of boosting self-esteem in youth. They argue that charity-oriented service risks promoting "one thousand points of status quo" rather than encouraging caring attitudes toward others and fostering commitment to enact social justice (16).

Placing an emphasis on the personal benefits of service detracts from the unique aspects that distinguish service as a pedagogical experience. Legislation to increase service opportunities specifies both personal and social benefits. For example, the National Community Service Act of 1990 listed the following benefits: "greater connection to the community, an easier transition from work to school, improved reliability, punctuality, and perseverance, development of self-esteem and sense of personal worth, and stronger basic skills and ability to work with others, and critical thinking" (U.S. Senate, 1990, 38). The distinguishing aspects of service are lost in this laundry list of benefits. Service is not unique in providing the opportunity to improve reliability, punctuality, self-worth, basic skills, and critical thinking. Part-time work or apprenticeship programs can promote the same personal benefits.

What service can uniquely provide for youth are opportunities for growth in moral, social, and civic awareness. In performing meaningful service, youth often engage in activities that probably are not directly connected to their future work aspirations. As the St. Francis students indicated, service has a much broader role. It helped them to understand their lives in relation to others and fostered the sense of being part of a historical process larger than themselves. Service activities sponsored by 4-H clubs and the Boy Scouts provide additional examples of organizations that combine service with worthwhile causes that can capture youth interests (e.g., Ladewig and Thomas, 1987).

3. Program Part of an Articulated Ideology One concern about the expanded implementation of service programs is that it will become just one more item on a list of requirements to earn a diploma, thus making it merely one more hurdle to jump. To avoid making school service an occasion for cynicism, it is important to be clear about the educational purpose of service and the ways it relates to other life experiences.

The St. Francis program countered cynicism by basing service on religious grounds that were integral to the school's mission. As a parochial school, St. Francis had a mission statement that articulated a definite ideological perspective on education. This statement articulates the goal of creating a Christian community that respects cultural and intellectual diversity, values service, promotes academic accomplishment, and nurtures students, faculty, and staff.

The service program was therefore a logical manifestation of a core part of this statement. While this formal mission statement was freely accessible to parents, students, and teacher, it was communicated in more concrete ways through a series of special events held throughout the year. Many of these events were organized by the teachers who worked hard to extend the experience of serving at the soup kitchen beyond the walls of the religion classroom. One way of doing this was to display visual reminders of the school's commitment to serving homeless people. Signs were placed throughout the school; for example, the name of the soup kitchen was painted on the wall of a major corridor, and student posters and collages on homelessness were displayed in the front entrance for one week, twice in the fall and once in the spring. Posters for the Thanksgiving food drive included statements such as "Give from the heart," "Give, nobody wants to be hungry," "Help by giving," and "Feed the hungry as ourselves." Other posters incorporated the name of the school mascot, with statements such as "[St. Francis mascot] means giving," and "St. Francis [mascot] is the food drive." As another visual reminder of the school's connection to the soup kitchen, photographs of students at the soup kitchen were included in the yearbook and in slide shows shown at beginning- and end-of-year assemblies and on parents' night.

The example of St. Francis brings into question the effectiveness of programs that treat service as just one of many academic requirements. It challenges programs that are not structured within an explicit ideological framework of, for example, a religious institution or movement-based organization to articulate clearly the overarching values represented by service participation. This is a particular challenge in the current context of diversity that marks the public educational system.

In her writings on public school reform, Fine (1991) shows one way in which service could be understood as part of the mission of public education as a community- and advocacy-oriented institution. Fine describes how in a public school setting, where sides are usually not taken, important social issues can still be addressed by reviewing the several sides that impinge on them. Not stating an opinion does not have to mean that all opinions cannot be articulated and discussed. In a similar fashion to the St. Francis discussion groups, one can imagine encouraging students to voice and debate their opinions so that all views are heard.

For Fine, service is part of a comprehensive plan to reform public education in the United States. It is a piece of a larger puzzle. We believe that whether a service program is implemented in a private or public school or as part of a community organization, it should be connected to the defining goals of the sponsoring institution. Furthermore, this connection needs to be instantiated not just in a formal mission statement but also in the daily practices of the sponsoring institution. This recommendation does not mean that all students will or should unquestioningly adopt the ideology. The St. Francis discussion groups indicated that students debated and struggled to make sense of the ideas that were presented in class. The ideology of social justice at St. Francis provided a framework on which students could build as they proceeded toward adulthood.

4. Activities Performed as a Group Another defining characteristic of the St. Francis program was that students performed service as an identifiable group. From the simple fact of arriving at the kitchen at approximately the same time and working together, to being recognized as partaking in an 18-year-old St. Francis tradition, the students were able to couple their individual identity with a clear sense of group. External supports were provided at the kitchen in signs and gestures that explicitly recognized this tradition. For instance, school bumper stickers were on the wall, and diners and staff members asked casual questions or made comments about the school, the athletic team, and the social justice class.

Interviews with civil rights participants conducted by McAdam (1988) and Fendrich (1993) support the importance of group awareness. These studies indicate that being part of a group can intensify the short- and long-term commitment of individual participants, even after the group disperses.

This idea contradicts the recommendation of some educators and policy makers, who state that youth should be given a choice of service activities so that experience is made to match their needs and personal dispositions (Kropp, 1994). There is obvious value to recognizing that individuals differ in being suited for particular kinds of tasks. But any advantage from that should be weighed against the additional benefit that comes from having students work together on a common project. The St. Francis students viewed their service at the soup kitchen as part of a common project. They knew that it was part of a tradition at the school that was equivalent to a rite of passage for juniors. Having students come together and share their experiences in group discussions no doubt reinforced this notion. In the discussion sessions, students talked about the junior year being the right time for them to go to the soup kitchen because they believed that they were now mature enough to handle its challenges and make a contribution.

5. *Reflective Opportunities with Peers* Empirical studies strongly support the idea of supplementing service with academic components and reflective opportunities (Cognetta and Sprinthall, 1978; Conrad and Hedin, 1982; Hamilton and Fenzel, 1988; Rutter and Newmann, 1989; Schlosberg, 1991). Policy advocates have adopted a similar outlook (Corporation for National and Community Service, 1994). Participants need to be prepared for their service and have opportunities to be debriefed and reflect on experience afterward. School-based programs often include reflective opportunities in the form of a personal journal and essays such as those required at St. Francis (Newmann and Rutter, 1983). While the format of written assignments varies, students are typically required to submit their writings to teachers for feedback in the form of comments rather than grades. It is clear in our data that essays provided a productive way for students to reflect on their experiences.

We also found that peer discussion groups can have an important pedagogical function. These discussions allowed students to participate in a joint process of thinking through questions stimulated by experiences at the soup kitchen. This public process complemented and extended the reflections in students' private essays. Talking together, students challenged and elaborated on one another's ideas in exchanges that led to consensual validation.

These discussion sessions also reinforced collective membership among the students. Students discovered that their peers had similar feelings and ideas about their time at the kitchen, and this realization helped to bolster group cohesion. Students learned that their peers shared their sense of moral indignation about conditions at the soup kitchen and other related social issues. They helped each other to define more precisely the sources of their indignation and possible courses of action.

6. *Program Organizers Serve as Models and Integrators* People who organize service and work with youth have an important opportunity to educate adolescents through their own example. Although some students at St. Francis disliked Mr. Siwek's demanding and opinionated manner, most expressed respect for him because they believed he was someone who lived his message. For instance, they knew that for five years Mr. Siwek had lived in a spiritually based community that ran a shelter and a soup kitchen, and they knew that for 15 years he had organized the Sunday meal at the soup kitchen. While students learned in their text about other exemplars of service, including public figures, Mr. Siwek was an accessible exemplar with whom they could interact on a daily basis. They learned through him that becoming a teacher was one route to helping *others* and that even those who care deeply about other people have good and bad days, optimistic and pessimistic moods.

Ms. O'Connell, who taught one of the six sections, was also well qualified to teach social justice. She had been active in service since high school and after college spent time doing volunteer service in Calcutta. Despite these qualifications, as a newcomer to the school, Ms. O'Connell had to establish her credibility with the students. In early discussion groups, students expressed regret that they did not have Mr. Siwek, the teacher who had developed the course. As the year progressed, Ms. O'Connell became increasingly involved in the school, organizing a weekend club for female students on probation and coaching an athletic team. She also volunteered at the soup kitchen on school holidays. These actions reflecting commitment toward the school and community service contributed to the increasing admiration that students expressed toward her as the year progressed.

It seems likely that teachers such as Mr. Siwek and Ms. O'Connell play a crucial role in a program's success. Their passion and dedication motivated and unified students. Both teachers were accessible role models of lifetime commitment to service. It seems relevant that alumni recollections of service at the soup kitchen and the social justice course made frequent reference to how they believed their lives had met or failed to meet the ideals established in Mr. Siwek's class.

Although some alumni articulated positions different from Mr. Siwek's, they still judged themselves relative to his criteria. This finding is suggestive of the lasting impact that dedicated service organizers can have.

7. Site Supervisors Serve as Models People who work at service sites provide another excellent and underappreciated resource. In the same way as service organizers, they can be models of moral commitment who offer their perspective on social problems and the dynamics of trying to alleviate these problems. While the ability of staff members to be educators may be limited by constraints of time and resources, this potential should not be overlooked when service organizers select sites and establish relationships with the staff at these sites.

St. Francis provides a good example of a program in which the people working at the service site took on the role of educators. On numerous occasions, while making sandwiches or cutting vegetables, students talked with kitchen staff about issues such as the increasing number of people coming to eat at the soup kitchen and the gentrification of the soup kitchen neighborhood. Students also asked staff members about their own lives, how they came to work at the soup kitchen, and why they had chosen a life with little material reward. For example, in her first essay one student gave this account of a conversation with a staff worker:

> As I was preparing what seemed like two million sandwiches, I began talking with Jennifer, who lives in a house with other people who run the kitchen. I asked her why she wanted to do that, because she was young. She asked me why I chose to ignore the problems of the poor. I told her I did not choose to ignore anything, but I was not choosing to devote my life to it. She understood, she smiled, and that was when I understood why she directed her life to the poor. As I was serving the soup and looking into these people's eyes, I was wondering why they were not saying "Thank you." Then I realized that they were so hurt and beaten down that they could not be thankful for the way I am. They are experiencing a whole other thanks. The thanks for waking up in the morning, the thanks for not being arrested, the thanks that they found a bed the night before. The people at the soup kitchen made me realize a new kind of thanks.

In this way, conversations with staff conducted in the context of serving homeless individuals encouraged students to reflect seriously on the connection between their soup kitchen experience and future life choices.

Mr. Siwek encouraged the involvement of staff as educators by maintaining communication during the year—speaking regularly with the staff on the phone and visiting the soup kitchen. He also invited the staff to speak at the Thanksgiving and end-of-year assemblies. To give the staff a better sense of the service program, he sent them copies of the students' essays about the soup kitchen. Staff members told us that reading the essays made them feel that they were part of an important experience for the students and increased their level of support for the program. On receiving the essays, staff members doubled their efforts to ensure that students were given occasions to interact directly with the people they served.

Essays and discussion groups indicate that students paid attention to the staff's treatment of the diners and how they ran the soup kitchen. They were critical of staff members when they were judged to have acted disrespectfully toward homeless individuals and when the quality of the food preparation was found wanting.

The example of St. Francis supports Newmann and Rutter's (1983) decision to include "working closely with adults" as part of their list of developmental opportunities (2). The Alliance for Service-Learning in Education Reform (1993) also lists skilled adult guidance and supervision as a standard for quality service programs. Clearly, the people with whom youth work during their service play a critical role in producing effects in the participants. The St. Francis students benefited from working with several adults who treated them with respect, took an active interest in their involvement, and frankly shared their own experiences of service.

8. Acknowledge Participants' Diversity The literature on community service describes the importance of planning programs that are developmentally appropriate and build on individual participant strengths. For example, the Corporation for National and Community Service (1994) recommends drawing "on the unique qualities of participants: their abilities, professional education or training, age, diversity, idealism, intelligence, and other assets" (4). We elaborate on this idea by pointing out that diversity among participants, service organizers, the staff at the site, and recipients can create potentially uncomfortable situations that require acknowledgment and support.

The literature on community service does not address how the dynamics of race, class, gender, and religion can influence service experience. In the St. Francis program, all of these issues were salient and created a degree of discomfort for participants. In discussion groups, some students indicated conscious awareness that their own minority racial status influenced their experience at the soup kitchen, which served a primarily minority population. Students were, for example, very upset by the large number of young black men who were in line for food and whom they compared with friends, relatives, and themselves. On several occasions students encountered acquaintances, relatives of friends, and even their own relatives in the food line. In addition, in trying to understand the situations of the homeless, students sometimes drew on personal experiences in which they had suffered discrimination themselves.

Some students were being asked to volunteer time for people whose economic situations were not far removed from their own. The recognition by students of how close they were to the edge of poverty may have helped them to be more empathic to those they served, but it was painful as well. In fact, some students said that requiring youth who were not economically well off to volunteer for disadvantaged populations was like "throwing it in [their] face." They argued that service initiatives should focus on middle- and upper-class youth. Adding further complexity to the issue of class, students were often distressed by the preconceptions of homeless people who treated them as if they were rich and spoiled because they went to parochial school.

The issue of gender was important in different ways for the male and female students. For the male students the activity of preparing and serving food had disturbing gender implications; some felt it was "female" work. For the female students, tensions sometimes arose because the soup kitchen served a primarily middle-aged male population. It was not uncommon for men to flirt with the female students and pressure them for dates or phone numbers. These young female adolescents were confused about how to respond to such advances. They were concerned about prejudging and hurting the men's feelings, but at the same time felt the advances were inappropriate and were frightened by them. In one incident, a female student gave her phone number to a man whom she subsequently learned from a staff member had attacked two women at a homeless shelter. After learning this, the student did not come to school for a week. She wrote in that quarter's essay that she felt she had acted stupidly and was angry at herself and frightened that the man would contact her.

The discussion groups provided a forum for students to talk about uncomfortable experiences and get feedback from their peers. It was within this context that students initiated discussion about the phone number incident and debated how one should respond to a diner who asks for a date or an address. Through their active participation in these exchanges, students signified that they wanted more opportunities to discuss these types of experiences. The examples from the St. Francis data show that educators and service organizers should not ignore the importance of race, class, and gender in designing programs. They should anticipate their saliency by addressing them, so as to turn uncomfortable situations into occasions for learning and broadening students' understanding of themselves and others.

9. Encourage a Sense of Being a Part of History As we have proposed throughout this chapter, service can have a powerful impact on youth's identity development when it fosters a sense of connection to society and larger historical processes. Research on participation in the civil rights movement (Fendrich, 1993, and McAdam, 1988) and the Peace Corps (Stein, 1966) has shown that youth become invested in service when they believe their actions are helping to make history. On the other hand, it is also easy to understand how youth can maintain the disengaged role of voyeur when service is treated as an isolated or decontextualized event.

Three characteristics of the St. Francis program helped to foster a sense of historicism. First, the course curriculum emphasized that students' actions were part of a historical religious perspective. Applying Catholic principles, particularly as articulated in the work of twentieth-century theologians Karl Rahner and Pierre Teilhard de Chardin, Mr. Siwek told students that they were part of an evolutionary process moving humanity closer to God. He argued that by doing something that was not the contemporary norm, such as becoming people who care about homelessness, students were moving all of humanity forward.

Second, much of the course content consisted in the history of activist movements in the United States. Moral exemplars were presented as historical figures who were ahead of their time and pushed humanity forward. Students learned about Martin Luther King's leadership in the civil rights movement, Cesar Chavez's struggle to improve the conditions of farm laborers, and Mitch Snyder's efforts to bring the plight of the homeless into the nation's consciousness. Mr. Siwek placed significant emphasis on Martin Luther King, Jr., who he said had a profound impact on his own life. In so doing, he offered a model from the recent history of blacks in the United States to encourage students to become part of a tradition of activism.

A third characteristic of the program that helped students to feel part of a historical process was the long-term relationship between St. Francis and the soup kitchen. For 18 years, students from St. Francis have performed the same service at the same soup kitchen, although it changed geographic location in the late 1980s. In this way, the experience of members of individual junior classes was a tangible part of the school's lore. Articulating this view, one student wrote at the end of her final essay in May: "There was no best moment for me today. Every moment I spent there, I spent as my last representation to St. Francis."

10. Acceptance of Responsibility The concept of responsibility resonated throughout the year in the St. Francis program. Classroom discourse, students' essays, and discussion groups all explored questions of personal and social responsibility. In the classroom, Mr. Siwek worked to make responsibility the primary theme of his course. The course textbook included the following statement on the course philosophy: "In the final analysis, either we care about these problems or we do not. If you do care, then you will want to know more, to be informed, to be able to think critically, and thus be prepared to make your response to this world." To add authoritative power, on the bottom of the same page, he placed an excerpt from Martin Luther King's final sermon: "For when people get caught up with that which is right, and they are willing to sacrifice for it, there is no stopping point short of victory" (King, 1986, 281).

One way Mr. Siwek kept the theme of responsibility present throughout the year was by emphasizing lines from videos shown during class. As one example, while the class viewed a "60 Minutes" segment on declining services for the homeless, Mr. Siwek paused the tape to emphasize a statement made by the commentator. Standing next to the video monitor, Mr. Siwek stated, "This is a line that you must memorize, 'A society is really judged by how it treats its least desirable people.' Not by its highways. No."

Students did not simply accept Mr. Siwek's interpretation of social problems; rather their essays and discussion groups reveal that they actively struggled with notions of responsibility. The following excerpt from an essay illustrates the complexity of thoughts and emotions concerning issues of responsibility evoked by service at the soup kitchen. This essay portrays a student's effort to integrate ideas from the soup kitchen, class, and previous personal experiences:

I was told "Thank you" over and over again. Really, that's about the only time that I felt like I was doing something right, except for a long time ago when I taught a lady's daughter on the bus how to say her ABCs. Everyone on the bus was smiling at me and clapping. And I felt like these people were clapping for me too, but in a different way. . . . I grew up around [streets in an impoverished inner-city area]. My life was "eat this, eat that, don't waste s—." But some how and some way we made it out. We went from a filthy apartment littered with vermin to a nice house [in a middle-class neighborhood]. But I just can't seem to figure out where we got the break. But who is going to give them a break? . . . But it was more than an assignment. It was a face to face meeting with reality. Now I see why you can't be a 5, even a 3, 4, 6, 7, 8, 9, or 2. There should be only ones or tens [an idea Mr. Siwek discussed in class]. If you are going to accept something, you should accept it wholeheartedly. But if you don't like it, then have the guts to come out and say it. . . . I'm still in-between. But me being in-between ain't going to help the world any. What I do know is that people shouldn't just sit back and let this happen.

This student's experiences at the soup kitchen caused him to find a meaningful response to the moral dilemmas of poverty and inequity. The fate of less fortunate others is no longer a distant issue. His essay describes a process through which questions of responsibility took on greater importance as they became increasingly personalized.

Conclusion

The ideas outlined in this chapter emphasize the fundamental need to implement service-learning programs in a coherent and integrated way. From the outset, service organizers should clarify the educational purpose of their program and develop it in accordance with this purpose. We believe that a major aim of current efforts to promote service-learning programs is to offer youth opportunities to feel connected to the broader society and make meaningful contributions for which they are respected. Underlying these efforts perhaps is the sense that current U.S. society offers youth few opportunities to experience societal connectedness and social responsibility (Youniss and Yates, 1997).

The service-learning program described in this chapter promotes identity development through its choice of service activity, curriculum, and explicitly integrated school activities. The program is a logical extension of the school's mission to promote service to others and social responsibility. Students are asked to identify with a tradition of service, a tradition made all the more profound because St. Francis students have served as a group at the same service site for the past 18 years. Service at the soup kitchen as part of a year-long course on social justice has encouraged students to become active members in their school and community and helped them to understand the bonds between the school and community. Students emerge from the year with a deeper awareness of social injustice, a greater sense of commitment to confront these injustices, and heightened confidence in their abilities overall. In this way, the program encourages precisely the forms of civic engagement and participation vital to a growing democracy.

References

Alliance for Service-Learning in Education Reform. 1993. Standards of quality for school-based and community-based learning. *Equity and Excellence in Education*, 26: 71–73.

The Baltimore Sun. Editorial. 1996. Clock ticking on "service learning." March 21, 16A.

Bullock, S. G. 1996. Public service, or else. *The New York Times*, May 16, A25.

Cognetta, P. V., and N. A. Sprinthall. 1978. Students as teachers: Role taking as a means of promoting psychological and ethical development during adolescence. In N. A. Sprinthall and R. L. Mosher (Eds.), *Value development as the aim of education*. Schenectady, N.Y.: Character Research Press.

Commission on National and Community Service. 1993. *What you can do for your country*. Washington, D.C.: Commission on National and Community Service.

Conrad, D., and D. Hedin. 1982. The impact of experiential education on adolescent development. In D. Conrad and D. Hedin (Eds.), *Child and Youth Services*, Special Issue: Youth Participation and Experiential Education, 4: 57–76.

Corporation for National and Community Service. 1994. *Principles for high quality national service programs*. Washington, D.C.: Corporation for National and Community Service.

Erikson, E. 1968. *Identity: Youth and crisis*. New York: Norton.

Fendrich, J. 1993. *Ideal citizens*. Albany: State University of New York Press.

Fine, M. 1991. *Framing dropouts: Notes on the politics of an urban public high school*. Albany: SUNY Press.

Flott, A. 1996. It's not true learning. *Omaha World Herald*, March 17, 14B.

Grotevant, H. G. 1993. The integrative nature of identity: Bringing the soloists to the choir. In J. Kroger (Ed.), *Discussions on ego identity*. Hillsdale, N.J.: Erlbaum.

Hamilton, S., and M. Fenzel. 1988. The impact of volunteer experience on adolescent social development. *Journal of Adolescent Research*, 3: 65–80.

Inhelder, B., and J. Piaget. 1958. *The growth of logical thinking from childhood to adolescence*. New York: Basic Books.

Kahne, J., and J. Westheimer. 1996. In the service of what? The politics of service learning. *Phi Delta Kappan*, 74: 593–599.

King, M. L., Jr. 1986. A testament of hope: The essential writings of Martin Luther King, Jr. In J. M. Washington (Ed.), *A testament of hope: The essential writings of Martin Luther King, Jr.* San Francisco: Harper and Row.

Kropp, A. J. 1994. Kids need responsibility. *USA Today,* April 20, 12A.

Ladewig, H., and J. K. Thomas. 1987. *Assessing the impact of 4-H on former members.* Research report. College Station: Texas A & M University.

Maddox, E. L. 1996. Del. Greenip right to attack service learning. *The Baltimore Sun,* February 6, 4C.

McAdam, D. 1988. *Freedom summer.* New York: Oxford University Press.

National and Community Service Coalition. 1995. *Youth volunteerism: Here's what the survey says.* Washington, D.C.: National and Community Service Coalition.

Newmann, F. M., and R. A. Rutter. 1983. *The effects of high school community service programs on students' social development: Final report.* Madison: University of Wisconsin Center for Educational Research.

Reinhard, J. 1996. Service learning: A symptom of American schools' decline. *Chapel Hill Herald,* March 17, 4.

Reuters News Service. 1997. Clinton asks nation's schools to promote volunteer service. *The New York Times,* April 6, A32.

Rutter, R. A., and F. M. Newmann. 1989. The potential of community service to enhance civic responsibility. *Social Education,* 53: 371–374.

Saunders, D. 1996a. Schools wrong to coerce student service. *Milwaukee Journal Sentinel,* July 29, 8.

Saunders, P. R. 1996b. "Slaves of state" in Bethlehem. *The Morning Call,* May 17, A22.

Schlosberg, A. 1991. Seven year follow up of an adolescent volunteer program in a psychiatric hospital. *Hospital and Community Psychiatry,* 42: 532–533.

Smith, L. 1997. Pride in service. *Los Angeles Times,* June 16, E1, E6.

Stein, M. I. 1966. *Volunteers for peace: The first group of Peace Corps volunteers in a rural community in Columbia, South America.* New York: Wiley.

Steirer, L. 1997. When volunteerism isn't noble. *The New York Times,* April 23, A23.

Strauss, V. 1994. In the spirit of Christmas: Private schools teach giving year-round. *The Washington Post,* December 25, A1, A8.

U.S. Senate Labor and Human Resources Committee. 1990. *Senate Report for National and Community Service Act of 1990.* Washington, D.C.

The Wirthlin Group. 1996. *The Prudential Spirit of Community Youth Survey.* Camden, N.J.: Prudential Life Insurance Company of America.

Yardley, J. 1986. How King changed our lives. *The Washington Post,* January 20, C2.

Yates, M. 1998 (in press). Community service and political-moral discussions among adolescents: A study of a mandatory school-based program in the United States. In M. Yates and J. Youniss (Eds.), *Roots of civic identity: International perspectives on community service and activism in youth.* New York: Cambridge University Press.

————, and J. Youniss. 1996a. Community service and political-moral identity in adolescents. *Journal of Research on Adolescence,* 6: 271–284.

————. 1996b. A developmental perspective on community service. *Social Development,* 5: 85–111.

Youniss, J., and M. Yates. 1997. *Community service and social responsibility in youth.* Chicago: University of Chicago Press.

Chapter 5

An Empowering, Transformative Approach to Service

Jeff Claus and Curtis Ogden

To become an integrated person is not only to understand the world in which we live and work, but to become the kind of person who will take part in shaping and reshaping those worlds. This emphasis on critique of current realities, and on participating in the re-creation of our worlds, is a central part of democratic life.
—Landon Beyer, *Creating Democratic Classrooms*

As the idea of service learning gains momentum and becomes more integrated into the life of schools and communities, we think it is important to continue thinking about what we hope to accomplish through service and what kinds of programs are most likely to help us achieve these goals. In a recent article, Stan Karp (1997) worries that the service-learning movement may become yet another "anemic" application of a potentially powerful idea. Similarly, Kahne and Westheimer (1996), Boyte (1991), and others (e.g., Jones, Maloy, and Steen, 1996; Lakes, 1996; Youniss and Yates, 1997) have cautioned us against adopting a "weak," "feel good," or "superficial" version of service. We share these concerns. Behind the belief that service work is a powerful pedagogical tool lurks the risk of rendering a complex activity banal through efforts to standardize and spread the service-learning movement. Service learning is not simply a pedagogical innovation rooted in the principles of experiential education and an interest in helping people and organizations in need. It also has the potential to become a transformative social movement, but this will only be realized if we view it as such.

Since 1992 the Learning Web, a community-based, youth-service agency in Ithaca, New York, has been the recipient of state and federal funds to run community-service programs for seventh through tenth graders in schools throughout its county. Both authors of this chapter have directed and been responsible for developing these programs.[1] During this time our thinking and program design have evolved toward an approach to service learning we think of as both empowering and transformative—empowering of youth and transformative of both youth and the society in which we live. We have worked to create circumstances in which youth are intrinsically motivated to reflect critically and to work together to improve their communities and the lives of people in them. In the process, youth appear to develop a wide array of skills and perspectives important both for living effectively in the world as it is currently constructed and for transforming the world into a better place. This, we feel, is an experience with implications not only for the individual development of participating youth but for the future of our society and world. From the perspective of our approach, individual development occurs as a consequence and within a framework of working to create a better world. It is closely linked to "the dream of changing the world, rather than adapting to it" (Freire, 1992, back cover).[2]

In this chapter we discuss some of what we think can and should be guiding principles for an empowering, transformative approach to service learning, and we describe a program we have developed for high school students in accordance with these ideas. By doing this we hope to encourage those involved in creating, running, and funding service programs to embrace the notion that service learning will be most motivating, meaningful, and effective for young people when it provides them with opportunities (i.e., when it empowers them) to define, investigate, think critically about, participate in, and act to improve the communities in which they live. We believe service learning has an extraordinary potential to engage young people in experiences involving explorations of community and self, critical thinking, democratic activism, and the pursuit of a more just and humane world. At its best, service learning can create circumstances in which young people develop a deeper understanding of their world and themselves and an improved sense of purpose, justice, agency, and optimism. It also provides them with tools for acting upon this understanding. Service-learning programs cannot achieve all of this, though, unless they are designed and carried out with these goals in mind.

The Principles of Empowering Education

Building on the ideas of Paulo Freire, John Dewey, and many others involved in the work of democratic, transformative education, Ira Shor, in his book *Empowering Education: Critical Teaching for Social Change* (1992), sets out a number of interwoven ideas we feel are particularly relevant to the task of developing an empowering, transformative approach to service learning. We would like to discuss five of these briefly here to create a framework for better understanding the design and philosophy of our program. These five concepts are *situated learning, dialogic discourse, teachers as problem posers, critical thought and consciousness,* and *activist learning.*

Situated learning means learning rooted in the lives, interests, themes, and concerns of the students. This approach to instruction makes the learning experience more personally meaningful and motivating than the traditional teacher-centered model, in which educators often "download" a predetermined curriculum. Shor describes this approach as fundamentally democratic. "To be democratic implies orienting subject matter to student culture—their interests, needs, speech and perceptions—while creating a negotiable openness in class where the students' input jointly creates the learning process" (Shor, 1992, 16). This, we think, is critical to achieving empowering service learning and is a key starting point and building block in the program we run. As we will discuss in detail below, our program allows students to determine their own group service projects on the basis of their evolving definitions of service, their interests, and an assessment of community needs. This helps develop a strong sense of ownership, motivation, and involvement in the varied work required to carry out a substantial service project.

Consistent with this idea is the concept of *dialogic discourse,* which means engaging students in a democratic, participatory process in which dialogue and group discussion are central to defining and negotiating the direction and progress of the learning experience. When applied to service learning this means participants work as a group and take an active role in discussing and deciding on the nature and path of the service activity. In the process they employ and develop democratic, group-process skills, which are fundamental to democratic decision making and success in the work of social reform.

The concept of *teachers as problem posers* encourages educators to generate critical, relevant, motivating questions, with and for students, and to use these questions to lead and frame the learning experience. In some cases these are the product of teacher-student dialogue and collaboration; in other instances they are provided by the teacher with an interest in helping students to become more aware of and to critically reflect on and question the world around them. When employed in service learning, this concept leads to a sequence of generating, investigating, and trying to answer critical questions that address issues and problems of interest to the participants and that are of significance to society. It means raising questions with young people about their community, for the purpose of generating and guiding investigation, reflection, dialogue, planning, and action. Through problem posing, service learning can become an experience of conducting critically reflective research which leads to community action.

Related to this idea is the concept of *critical thought and consciousness*. Without a critical, questioning perspective, Shor and many others argue, education supports the status quo and thus cannot be transformative. As a result, Shor encourages teachers to engage students openly and explicitly in analyzing, questioning, and rethinking important societal arrangements and structures, noting that without a critical perspective and awareness students will not be able to identify those aspects of society and their lives that will benefit from constructive change. He sees problem posing, dialogue, and critical thought or awareness as working together not only to raise important questions but to illuminate a path toward transformative action.

> Problem posing offers all subject matter as historical products to be questioned rather than as universal wisdom to be accepted. . . . In this democratic pedagogy, the teacher is not filling empty minds with official or unofficial knowledge but is posing knowledge in any form as a problem for mutual inquiry. (Shor, 1992, 32–33)

> When educators offer problem-posing, democratic dialogue in the classroom, they challenge socialization into the myths, values and relations of the dominant culture. . . . Critical teachers provide a social experience in education that questions previous experiences in school and society and that models new values, relationships, discourse, knowledge, and versions of authority. (Shor, 1992, 117–118)

> The basic process of dialogue—problem-posing—actively questions schooling, society, teacher-talk, and existing knowledge. It democratically invites students to make their education, to examine critically their experience and social conditions, and to consider acting in society from the knowledge they gain. (Shor, 1992, 188)

In service learning, critical consciousness or awareness is important because it informs and guides service in a way that the service can be transformative of the world rather than simply adaptive. Critical awareness takes students beyond the act of feeding those who are hungry to questioning why people are hungry and working to help the hungry feed themselves. This constitutes development of an analytical, reflective perspective that helps service participants better understand their world, with an eye for improving it.

Finally, *activist learning* means not just guiding students to question the past and present for the purpose of envisioning an improved future but actively pursuing reform on the basis of the knowledge gained through research and reflection. It means helping youth connect a critical perspective to social action in order to become agents of constructive change. Shor continues: "Activist learning is oriented to change-agency. Change-agency in this pedagogy means learning and acting for the democratic transformation of self and society. . . . [It means] actively studying life to change it" (Shor, 1992, 190–192). Or, as Sorensen (1996) writes, "Decision making, critical thinking, reflection, and recognizing multiple viewpoints are all part of the process of empowerment. However, empowerment cannot be achieved without action. . . . Empowerment involves action; action involves change. Empowered individuals work to make meaningful changes to benefit their community" (91).

What this means for service learning is that it should be centered, from the outset, around the pursuit of constructive change. Questioning, dialogue, planning, reflection, and action should all be framed by the purpose of achieving meaningful reform. This is at the heart of the potential power in service, as youth can be given an opportunity to critique, plan, and act in personally relevant ways to improve their communities and world. Thus, what otherwise might be viewed as an adaptive act of service becomes a transformative step in community development. In the process, young people often develop a sense of agency and optimism, a hopefulness, about their capacity to realize their own visions for a better world.

Taken together these concepts suggest an approach to service learning that begins with student-derived interests and perspectives; proceeds with dialogue, research, and critical thought; and leads to social action and ongoing reflection.[3] This, we think, is what empowering, transformative service learning is all about. Ultimately, it is this guided process that creates for youth a view that change is possible and that they can play an important role in achieving it.

ImPACT: The Learning Web Approach

During the past five years, the Learning Web has developed and run an extracurricular community service program that it offers on a rotating basis to the county's middle and high schools. At the high school level the program is called ImPACT, which stands for the Importance of Participating, Acting, and Coming Together. Initially focused on small schools in rural communities, the program has recently expanded to include a larger city high school as well. Each project ultimately consists of a Learning Web staff person, one or two college interns, about 8–12 student volunteers, and a handful of teachers and school staff who come together to create a service initiative that we hope will lead to self-sustained service activity in the future.

In all of its programs the Learning Web works closely with schools to provide interested youth with experiential learning opportunities. A central objective of the organization is to help youth develop the skills necessary to be more self-directed in their learning and lives. As Learning Web founder Michelle Whitham wrote in 1976, the organization "attempts to facilitate the decisions that its clients make about what they want to take place . . . rather then requiring each student to participate in a pre-designed curriculum. . . . In other words, the students direct their own experiences" (21).

In accordance with this philosophy, the Learning Web gives young people in its community-service programs the opportunity to determine what their projects will be and how they will be carried out. We begin this process as we recruit volunteer after-school groups, presenting information, generating discussion, and soliciting participation in high school classrooms. From the outset, including during the recruitment phase, we engage young people in reflecting on and discussing their lives, communities, and views of service. We feel these discussions allow young people to construct personally meaningful definitions of service and community, and they motivate youth to get and stay involved and to pursue action of significance to them. This approach also introduces potential volunteers to the youth-centered, participatory nature of the program and helps guide eventual project planning.

Initial Steps in the Youth-Centered Approach

One of the main questions we pose and pursue in the recruitment and initial phases of the program is, "What is community service?" The ensuing discussions and comments usually reveal a range of experiences with and perceptions of service, from the sophisticated and enthusiastic to the limited and negative. On the negative end, for example, we sometimes hear comments such as these: "Community service is usually just picking up garbage. That's so boring." "Community service is for kids who've gotten in trouble."

At this stage we acknowledge all relevant feelings and reactions and encourage a discussion of what community service could and should be. In association with negative views, a question often raised is, "*Why should I get involved in community service?*" Rather than answering this for young people, we let dialogue be our guide. We make clear that the program is an opportunity for young people to define community service in ways they find meaningful and to pursue community action they feel is valuable. If we simply refuted negative perceptions of service, we feel we would risk invalidating real experiences that can be fertile ground for reflection and, ultimately, committed participation. Some very lively conversations about what community service should be have grown out of recruiting sessions, and we think these are productive. In this way we try to go where young people *are* rather than ask them to come to us.

As part of this process of situating community service in the experiences of young people, we often use an exercise in which we ask students to study a list of about a dozen activities that could be defined as community service, then to rank them in terms of their own ideals. There are always differences in response, even in the smallest group, and these are an excellent source of discussion and reflection. Some people, for example, choose "talking with a friend" as their ideal, while others may put this last. Some people pick "riding your bike to work and leaving the car at home," while others roll their eyes. Many choose "cooking a meal for the homeless," while "joining the armed forces" is often a controversial choice. Differences in experience and values quickly become apparent, and discussion of these differences generally leads to a broader understanding and definition of community service, reflective of social and cultural aspects of the students' lives and their views of community need. When we ask young people to boil all of this down to a basic definition, it generally reveals that everyone thinks that community service should be about helping others or contributing to the common good, including striving for positive change. This, in turn, opens up conversation about what they, as young people, would like to see done in their communities.

During recruitment, we have also made it a practice to bring along former youth program participants to share some of their experiences with the program and the service projects they have done. This peer-to-peer sharing often proves to be a powerful motivational tool and a further contribution to the pool of project possibilities. At this point we attempt to elicit some concrete examples of activities we might undertake, and we distribute a sign-up list for those who are interested in taking the next step.

The next step is an after-school meeting during which we show and discuss a video about young people throughout the United States taking the initiative to get involved in their communities.[4] This video was produced by, with, and for teens and young adults, a fact that always catches the attention of our youth audience. It is common for viewers, after watching the film, to comment that although they like the video it has little to do with issues in their community. This too, then, becomes a launching point for critical group reflection and discussion about their communities, issues that are important to them, and ways in which they might address some of these issues.

Students generally respond positively to these sessions. We think this is because they are given an opportunity to reflect critically in a way that validates and shows respect for the knowledge and insight they bring to the project. As one young woman commented in a final evaluation of the program, "One big reason I joined ImPACT was that you began by asking me my opinion. You really showed us that this was *our* project." Thus, before they have done anything project-oriented, students in the program engage in fundamental reflection that requires them to think about and define community service so it is meaningful to them and consistent with their experience, ideals, and concerns. In this way we attempt to both orient young people to service and orient service to the lives of young people. This, we believe, situates the work of the program in the culture of youth participants and sets the stage for meaningful action and learning.

Developing Deeper Connections to Service

We form/select a volunteer group that usually consists of 8–12 young people and is established to work together for about four to six months. In accordance with grant specifications, at least half of each group is made up of students who are identified as "at-risk" using criteria provided in the grant. Meetings are held twice a week after school for a total of about five hours of activity a week. We begin each group with discussions and exercises that focus on self-concept and are geared toward developing self-esteem and strengthening personal connections to the program's themes.

One of the first conversations we have with a new group centers around each individual's motivation and goals for joining the program.

In each group young people articulate a variety of reasons for getting involved, including altruism, an interest in doing something about some aspect of their community or society they feel needs attention, boredom, a desire for community and to be with peers after school, a desire to have a new experience, and resume building. Some youth have very specific goals and ideas from the outset, while others have trouble explaining why they have decided to join. At this point, we are most interested in maintaining dialogue as a guide and motivational tool.

Participants definitely learn about and influence each other constructively as they discuss why they have volunteered. We have also found that participants' goals change over the course of a project, and we want them to be aware of this evolution. Quite often they go from being interested primarily because they want to do something after school other than go home to watch television, to being genuinely concerned and reflective—sometimes passionate—about a social issue and/or an aspect of their community they want to address. We think helping youth become self-reflective about this kind of development can be an important part of developing critical awareness and a socially conscious sense of identity.

Another exercise we use early on with each group is to develop a skill or talent inventory of its members. This gives participants an opportunity to identify and share their individual strengths and interests and a chance to connect these to the future work of the project. Once we have generated a list of talents—a "group resume"—we ask how some of these talents might be applied to community service activity. For example, if someone in the group states that he or she is musically inclined, we ask how that skill might be used in a project. The same goes for those who say they are skilled in fixing cars or computers, working with people, gardening, writing, and so on. The idea we want to convey at this point is that service is not simply about joining conventional responses to perceived problems but can be more meaningful when people use their talents and creativity to dream up new approaches.

We also engage groups in exercises geared toward clarifying values and then follow up with discussions about how these values might affect their choice of projects. For example, having young people prioritize values at play in their own lives (financial security, love, personal safety, etc.) can help guide them in the selection of certain themes or issues they hope to address. This can raise awareness of the bigger picture behind service work. At times, these exercises will reveal contradictions between aspirations for one's self, such as wealth, and those for society at large, such as equity. Addressing these contradictions is a way to get young people to think critically, to reconcile individual and social goals, and to clarify visions for meaningful change. Another exercise we often use is called "Roles We Play." In it, members are asked to think about the roles they play in a given week (student, daughter, sister, friend, congregation member, Girl Scout). This helps explore individual connections to community and ways in which these relationships might lead to service options. It enlivens and expands a group's outlook, and it has proven especially useful and motivational in smaller communities where conventional service activities (often through institutional linkages) may not be so readily apparent or available.

It is also important to mention that in addition to holding group meetings, we often arrange an initial one-time or short-term service project for each new group to undertake after its first couple of weeks together. We have a connection with a local volunteer coordination service that organizes college students to do renovation work in the low-income and not-for-profit housing sector. Through them we set something up. This gives our group a real experience with volunteer service upon which we can reflect. *What did you think? Did you enjoy this project? Why or why not? Was it valuable, and, if so, in what ways? What community needs did the work address? Why do these needs exist? How else might you address these needs? What lessons can we take from this experience and apply to our own service work?* In this way, participants continue to develop a sense of their own visions of community service and to engage in discussions of how they would like to define and address their community's needs. These are, we think, important first steps in the process of pursuing empowering and transformative service and action.

The Value of Working in Groups

While we support the idea of having young people personalize the concept of service, we also want to be sure not to make it a selfish undertaking. In initial brainstorming sessions we sometimes hear suggestions of projects that are essentially self-serving ("let's organize a party") or lack meaning outside of the immediate group. This is when we move our focus from individual interests to community building. This can be achieved through questioning—"How will throwing a party contribute to the community's well being? Who will it help? How will it help them? What issues will it address?"—or the use of certain discussion tools, including quotes and poems.[5] It is important to situate service in the lives of young people, and it is equally vital to encourage work that is socially meaningful. Striking this balance is what our approach is all about, bringing together the processes of individual growth and community development.

Thus the fact that we work with *groups* of young people is very significant. Each group consists of a mix of students with regard to academic performance, social class, gender, ethnicity, and personality. Bringing together multiple outlooks and aspirations requires shared leadership and negotiation. This means that participants have to learn how to communicate, understand, respect, and get along with each other to carry out their service projects. Developing these skills is an integral part of Learning Web community service. As we say to each group, "If you want to help build community *out there*, you might as well begin *right here*."

Interpersonal issues often arise as part of this group-building process, and we make sure to engage young people in discussion about these issues and the differences in their lives. Issues of social class and school and community social structure, for example, must often be addressed before we can proceed in our work together. These issues thus become teachable moments that sometimes seem to take us far beyond the details of the task at hand, but not in an irrelevant way. They introduce some young people to issues of social justice they had not been objective about, even though the issues are a central part of their lives. Some groups have even decided to address these issues in their project work.

As the group settles into its routine, we engage participants in moving beyond individual identity to think about group identity. How do they want to function as a group? How will they make decisions? Where do they want to meet? How will meetings be facilitated? What is their agenda? How do they want to present themselves to the wider community? Answers to these questions develop over time and with practice as youth experiment with leadership and decision making. In the initial stages of each project, Learning Web staff play more of a facilitation role, but as time passes the young people generally become more active and take more responsibility as they learn appropriate skills and gain experience and confidence.

In addition to discussion and the practice of group facilitation, we introduce various exercises and activities designed to build trust within the group, to illustrate the importance of cooperation, and to train participants in the process of developing consensus. Cooperative problem-solving games emphasize the importance of listening, focus, synthesis, prioritization, and clear communication in successful group work. The next step is to take these skills out into the field, with the reminder that just as we must work cooperatively and respectfully within the group, we must apply these practices to the wider community of which we are all a part.

Community Investigation

Community investigation is another activity fundamental to our model for service learning. As already noted, we believe that giving young people the opportunity to identify and pursue their own projects helps them develop the tools to take initiative in the future. As the Zimbabwean proverb goes, "Spoonfeeding teaches one nothing but the shape of the spoon." Or, as Jerome Bruner writes, "Acquired knowledge is most useful to a learner . . . when it is discovered through the learner's own cognitive efforts, for it is then related to and used in reference to what one has known before" (1996, xii). A next important step in the process, then, is for the group to engage in community investigation and research that will help them make decisions about which service projects to pursue and how. This, too, encourages participants to move beyond their own immediate frames of reference to consider the needs of others and issues in the wider community and society.

When we speak of *community* for the purposes of our projects, we generally begin with the geographic school district in which we are operating, though this can be subdivided into neighborhoods or expanded to the county level. This exploration period allows participants to develop a meaningful context for any service project they carry out and deepens their understanding of possibilities for action. The group is ultimately guided by its collective interests and problem-posing techniques. It all begins with the questions "What are the components of a community and this community in particular?" and "How can we gather information that will help us pursue meaningful, effective action here?"

To begin to focus more intensely on the actual community, we use an exercise that asks participants to make lists of the five characteristics they think best describe their community, the five things they like most about their community, and the five things they like least about their community. Using these lists as a starting point, we brainstorm and discuss changes they would like to see made in their community, being sure to guide the group to identify both community assets and areas for improvement. This information becomes critical as the group progresses toward choosing issues to address. It also sets the stage for deeper investigation.

For purposes of gathering community information, we employ a variety of investigative techniques, with some suggested by the young people and others proposed by Learning Web staff. One thing we always do is introduce participants to anthropological perspective and method. Anthropology, and in particular the ethnographic method, does not seem to make its way into many middle and high school classrooms, although it is very useful in helping young people understand their communities and different people's experiences in them. A discussion of culture and social structure, and the ways in which they affect individual outlook and social interaction, can point to the importance of trying to see life through the eyes and experiences of others. This is helpful in developing both compassion and critical thought as young people learn to consider multiple perspectives and to raise questions about social problems as seen by others.[6]

The next component of the investigative stage is consideration of the community resources participants will tap to learn more about what is going on and what might be done in the future. This is most often done simply by asking youth to identify institutions, facilities, and people that exist in the community. Sometimes we break down the community into areas such as economy, politics, education, religion, culture and recreation, health, and social services to help guide young people's thinking. We also discuss power relationships within the community. *What is power? Who has power? What kind of power do they have? Who lacks power? What are the implications of power relationships for the way things are in their community and for how things get done?* Investigation is not just a question of discovering who lives in the community but of how these people relate to and interact with each other and where the young people themselves fit in.

Community investigations have taken many different forms. These include conducting observational walking tours in certain parts of the community; studying a map of the area and identifying key geographic features; gathering information through surveys and inventories; interviewing members of the community (both peers and adults) about social issues, history and project ideas; soliciting input from the community by putting notices about the group in local newsletters and newspapers; meeting with representatives of appropriate organizations and local government; and scanning local publications. In one community, group members came up with the idea of convening a forum of community leaders, during which they asked the leaders about pressing community issues and the potential role they saw young people playing to address them. In another community, the group handed out cookies at lunchtime in the school cafeteria in return for project ideas.

Something else that often happens at this stage is that we offer to take participants to visit a local service clearinghouse, Cornell University's Public Service Center (in Ithaca, where we are based), which publicizes local, national, and international volunteer opportunities. This trip to Cornell allows group members to ask a lot of questions, to learn about what makes a project successful and satisfying, and to look at concrete examples of initiatives taking place in other communities that they might want to adapt to their own surroundings.

Throughout this process participants are encouraged to determine the direction of the investigation, to make calls and arrangements, and to design and conduct interviews and other information-gathering activities. They work as a group to identify questions they would like to ask and have answered, and they conduct research. In addition, we engage participants in discussions of what they are experiencing and learning as they think about the future direction of the project(s). The guiding questions for this phase are, "What needs are there in the community?" "Whose needs are these?" "What are the sources or causes of these needs?" "How might we contribute to and help improve the community, by addressing some of these needs?" "What resources might we use/are available?" And, "What do we want to do as a group to act on answers to these questions?"

In postprogram evaluations, students generally comment on how much they enjoy this stage. They particularly like interviewing community members on subjects of interest to the group. These activities also tend to raise important social issues for discussion and debate, including hunger and homelessness, local and national health issues, funding for social programs, educational philosophy and practice, limited roles for young people, zoning practices, issues of race and class, and so on. We find that young people very much like thinking about and discussing major issues such as these when their views and ideas are taken seriously and have a purpose.

Decision Making

The community exploration phase of each project continues through the end of our time together as we keep our eyes and ears open to ongoing developments and opportunities; nevertheless, its primary purpose is to help the group select a project or projects to pursue. For this we use a democratic approach that centers around group discussion, reflection, and consensus. Not everyone has the same interests, but we try to prioritize, to focus on feasibility, and, if we decide to take on a number of projects, to address topics of interest to most members of the group.

In one community, for example, after interviewing teachers, parents, friends, and others and after much discussion, the group narrowed their project ideas to two. The group then visited the two possible sites to investigate further. First they went to a senior citizens' residence to talk to the manager and some of the residents about what the group might do there. On the basis of this visit and substantial discussion afterward, the group decided that opportunities for significant and satisfying contribution did not seem as promising there as they had hoped. They then visited a small, rundown park they were considering rehabilitating. While there they conducted a thorough inventory of what they thought needed repair. Next, after a discussion of what they might do in the park and how this would contribute to the community, they decided to put together a questionnaire and canvas the neighborhood near the park to find out how people used it and what they would like to see done to improve it. Then the students arranged a meeting with some members of the local government on a committee overseeing parks to discuss what permission they might need to go ahead with the project and how local officials might help the students accomplish their goals. Finally, after a good deal of reflection about service, the community, and what they hoped to accomplish in the group, the students decided democratically to undertake the park project.

In the process of community exploration, this group learned a great deal about their community and its issues, government, and citizens. They learned about their town's governmental structure, who occupied key positions in it, and how to engage these people. They also gained confidence in their ability to accomplish community service goals, coming to a new understanding of their power to work for change.

The projects we have completed over the years have varied greatly depending on the youth and community involved. Some groups have chosen long-term commitments, others a series of shorter projects. Some have decided to help existing initiatives, others have decided to start their own. To name a few of the projects worked on during our five years: groups have assisted with housing renovations for low-income families and nonprofit agencies; renovated rundown parks in neighborhoods with limited resources; helped nonprofit agencies with office work and fundraising; painted play equipment at a child care center; worked with senior citizens living in a retirement home; painted buildings at a community-owned fairground; planted trees in public settings with little landscaping; made and distributed food for a food pantry; worked with animals at the SPCA; picked up trash in yards and along roadways; contributed artwork to a community festival; reviewed youth grant proposals; produced a magazine about increasing youth participation in the community; organized a community concert with five bands to bring youth together, combat youth idleness, and raise funds for an organization supporting poor families; lobbied local government to create more avenues for input from young people; and drawn up a proposal for a youth center.

While some of these projects do not look much different from those of many other service groups, what is different is the process. In other words, while these may be conventional on the surface, they are more unconventional in substance, especially from the participants' point of view. For example, one group of youth began by expressing disdain for any project that might require them to pick up garbage. After a month of youth-led investigation, however, the first project the group selected was a clean-up of a local park. In the end, it was not a question of the activity itself but the meaning behind it. The group had time to discover connections between their own values and community needs and, therefore, did not see themselves as merely picking up garbage but as beautifying a place that was important to many people in the community and (in their words) "setting an example" for their peers. We feel this illustrates the importance of an empowering process, one that allows time for exploration and real decision making. As Bruner (1996) writes, "Educational encounters, to begin with, should result in understanding, not mere performance. Understanding consists in grasping the place of an idea or fact in some more general structure of knowledge" (xi, xii).

Purposeful Reflection

As we have written elsewhere (Ogden and Claus, 1997), we feel strongly that reflection is a critical part of substantive service learning. Without reflection there is little meaningful learning. We also believe that reflection is richer and more engaging for adolescents when it plays a functional, contributing role in the development and implementation of a community service project or work related to it—that is, when it is an integral, necessary part of the service process, as opposed to something that occurs somewhat artificially apart from service. This is what we call purposeful reflection, and it is our sense that this approach is more intrinsically motivating for young people and contributes to deeper critical awareness and concern.

Thus, as projects progress, we continue to engage participants in reflecting on their communities, lives, and service goals, paying close attention to opportunities to raise issues of social justice along the way. This helps participants find and create relevance in their work and to think critically about various aspects of their community and society as they work to improve them. The work of carrying out the project(s) can be a very powerful source of emotion and discussion, especially when it involves working with and for other people. As a result, we make sure to discuss what group members are doing and feeling as they perform their service work, whatever it may be. We do this both formally, as part of the ongoing planning and revising process, and informally, on trips to and from the service sites, and, when appropriate, during our work time together. This becomes a key way for group members to process their emotions and to contribute to the functioning and direction of the group.

During a project at a low-income senior citizens' home, for example, a couple of youth, on the trip home one day, commented that they had worked with a woman who seemed crabby and not appreciative of their presence and desire to help. The group immediately struggled to make sense of this. This provoked a discussion about how older people are viewed and treated in our society. For an hour we discussed how being treated as needy, because of your age and finances, might anger people who have been able-bodied and independent most of their lives. We talked about pride, respect, and what it means to grow old. We also discussed the limited finances of the people the students were working with and how this might affect their attitude toward society and the students themselves. This conversation welled up naturally from the emotions of the participants who had been moved by the experience, and then it was nurtured by Learning Web staff. Ultimately, it led to a more compassionate approach to their work with seniors, and it generated a broader interest in and awareness of issues of ageism and social policy for seniors.

Service can and should be used as a powerful vehicle for achieving a deeper kind of learning about and from others—others who may often be thought, by youth or in our society, not to have significant or important knowledge. This requires keeping an eye on possibilities for genuine two-way exchange between students and the people they interact with while providing service. With reflection, youth often come to the conclusion that they are receiving more than they are giving, and they develop a new understanding of and respect for those being served. An example of this is a small project in a rural community in which a group set out to help a visually impaired senior citizen save an old tree in her yard. In return for their efforts, the senior shared her jam-making skills with the young people, and, in turn, they produced a batch of strawberry jam, which they donated to the local food give-away. In reflective discussion during this interaction and afterward, many young people in the group came to the conclusion that the relationship between the server and the served is a complex, ambiguous, and ever-changing one that must be closely attended in order to achieve and maintain balance and a sense of pride for both. This experience truly played on everyone's strengths, leaving no one in the singular role of service provider or recipient.

We also encourage participants to keep written accounts of their service experience as part of the task of remembering and noting things the group may want to include in their own write-ups of their work or to communicate to the press. Writing often proves to be very functional in the life of a project as it finds its way into press releases, proposals, volunteer recruitment, and editorials. Related to this activity, we generally try to enlist local television and newspapers in reporting on a group's work as it is occurring. This allows us to engage group members in preparing to be covered by the media, which means having them think about what they would like to show and tell the journalists, what questions they think would be interesting questions to answer, and how they might answer likely questions. We also tell participants that expressing their views can be a form of service itself when it motivates others to take action or consider something from a new or different point of view.

It is part of the Learning Web's mission to build bridges between young people's work in the community and school by working with teachers to get participants credit or to create opportunities for class projects related to their experiences. This can be an empowering process in and of itself when young people have the courage to approach their teachers and suggest projects that they see as relating to a given subject matter. In the past, participants have been awarded credit for articles by English teachers, for creative reflection by art teachers, and for surveys and questionnaires by social studies and careers teachers. Creating these opportunities for credit can go a long way in motivating young people to reflect on their community service experiences and help them understand the connections between school and "the real world."

Another way of motivating young people to reflect is through written materials and speakers that address issues that crop up in the course of each project. These might include editorials, newspaper clippings, books, activists, and so forth. We encourage young people to bring in relevant resources as they come across them, and Learning Web staff occasionally distribute hand-outs or invite presenters with the blessing of group members. This can deepen our appreciation of certain issues at the local level or broaden and connect them to national and global happenings.

For example, in one rural school district, participants discovered that their town did not have much coherence or community spirit. As they interviewed residents about community issues and asked for suggestions on possible projects, they encountered considerable apathy and complaints that people did not really seem to care very much for the town. Part of the reason for this is that the town has no recognizable center. As one community member said, "This is like a rural residential strip mall. There really isn't any place to gather." This tended to carry over into most people's lack of enthusiasm about community service. The group elected to do a few small beautification projects and then heard about a local landscape architect who was interested in creating a town center by designing a town green. We invited her to talk with us about town planning and community development and about ways in which the group might contribute to creating more community spirit. Our session ended with the architect asking group members for ideas on the town center.

There are indeed many opportunities to weave reflection into the entire process of carrying out a project, and we view each of these as essential to helping young people deepen their awareness, widen their outlook, consider and respect other perspectives, inform their decisions, question their world, and develop a sense of agency.

Closure and Continuity

An important part of concluding a Learning Web service project is to have the group identify things they feel they have learned—about themselves, others, their service, and their community—and to have them communicate this both within and beyond the group. This work involves both evaluative reflection and the defining of possible future action. By the end of a project, many participants develop insights into the workings and needs of their community that they want to share with others. Groups often, for example, create a list of tasks or activities that they had hoped to complete but must leave unfinished, and they identify additional community needs they would like to see addressed. Participants also often want to encourage members of their community to volunteer service time and effort as they themselves have done. These ideas are then presented to appropriate officials and community members, sometimes in the form of written lists and proposals, sometimes in the form of newspaper articles or letters to the editor. As mentioned earlier, participants in past projects have actually assisted with the recruitment phase at other schools by sharing their experiences and opinions and encouraging their peers to get involved. Some participants have also been involved in giving presentations at youth leadership conferences, to local youth commissions, and in college education classes.

Additionally, we ask participants at the end of a project to help us improve our running of the program by filling out an evaluation form. Here, too, we are able to engage the group in thinking and talking about their experience, this time as they work to help us do a better job in the future. We ask them questions about the quality of the program and about their experience and sense of growth in it. We also ask them to help us develop more ideas for making the program appealing to other youth, and we ask them to tell us what we should say to potential participants to help them understand what they might get out of the experience.

We also work as a group to plan a celebration of what has been accomplished and experienced. We allow the group to plan their own celebration, with the stipulation that the event somehow be related to their service efforts and not just be a self-serving party. The group that rehabilitated the park, for example, had a picnic at the park to which they invited local officials, some people from the neighborhood, and a few friends. At this gathering the group reviewed and showed what they had done and presented to local officials a list of things they had not had time or resources to complete. They secured a promise that the work would continue. They also hung a sign with the name of the park, having the mayor hammer in the last nail, and they had pizza, chicken, cake, and soda, some of which had been solicited from and donated by local businesses. In addition, they were presented with individual awards of recognition from the local government.

In all of the programs we have facilitated, at least some of the students in each group conclude they want to continue being involved in community service work. In three instances this has meant that students, with our help, have worked to create a service group that would live beyond the term of the Learning Web program. To accomplish this, the students had to seek out resources and support from their schools or appropriate youth programs, and they did their own recruiting. Much of this desire to continue in service work can be credited to the youth themselves, though we also see the process of tool building and self-direction employed throughout our program as a vital impetus for sustained activity. We have found that young people in our programs have a heightened awareness of where to turn to keep things going and the confidence to get some of this done themselves. A number of times a group of young people we recruited has turned around at the end of our time together and recruited their own adult advisor (whether a teacher, youth worker, or parent).

Throughout the past few years we have also held numerous reunions and retreats, which bring members of these older and still-functioning groups together with our students in current programs to discuss issues and take on big projects. This has forged a countywide network of youth who support and inspire one another across community boundaries through shared stories and collaboration. Furthermore, many of these young people have had opportunities to attend state and national conferences on service learning and community building, where they meet their peers and observe both the diversity and the common themes in this youth movement. In the process, their developing excitement for acting on the world in critically reflective ways is supported and reinforced.

Conclusion

Having witnessed the richness of service that aims to empower young people, we are concerned that service learning may become "just another graduation requirement," often failing to engage youth fully in a mix of critical reflection and democratic action. To counter this possibility, we encourage use of a student-centered, activist approach, which, we feel, makes service more motivating, meaningful, and substantive for youth and promises fuller and more truly democratic participation in the pursuit of constructive social change. We embrace the view that "schools and classrooms"—and, we add, communities—"should be laboratories for a more just society than the one we now live in. Unfortunately, too many schools [and communities] are training grounds for boredom, alienation, and pessimism. . . . Classrooms [and communities] can be places of hope, where students and teachers gain glimpses of the kind of society we could live in and where students learn the academic and critical skills needed to make it a reality" (Bigelow et al., 1994, 4).

This view sometimes takes us into risky territory, because it makes a clear choice concerning the role of education in our society. It acknowledges, in fact embraces, the reality that all education is political activity—that there is no neutral or apolitical education—and it argues for viewing schools and educational programs as agents of change and social justice rather than instruments of social control and the status quo. This opens the door to conflict, but in this risky zone lie the promise and optimism of youth and adults *engaged in*, not alienated from, society as they pursue the improvement of their communities and issues of social justice. As Bruner (1996) writes, "Education is risky, for it fuels the sense of possibility. But a failure to equip minds with skills for understanding and feeling and acting in the cultural world is not simply scoring a pedagogical zero. It risks creating alienation, defiance, and practical incompetence. And all of these undermine the viability of a culture" (42–43).

Thus, a strong, democratic version of service learning is, we think, the best choice for the development of youth, our communities, and society. It promises engagement over alienation, and it places at least one element of education in the position of being the head of the societal dog instead of the tail.

We would also like to draw attention to what we think is the value of community-based organizations in providing this kind of service learning. Community-based organizations often occupy positions in their communities that allow them a unique perspective and capacity for guiding youth in community exploration, critical reflection, and the pursuit of community/social change. Community-based organizations can develop programs and provide services that are particularly capable of bridging school and community and of raising and addressing issues relevant to both. Recently, for example, the Learning Web was invited to offer ImPACT as part of a special program for "at-risk" youth in a local high school. Under this arrangement, Learning Web staff teach ImPACT as a class two days a week and work with a team of teachers to integrate reflection into other subject areas. As we move through the school year, we identify themes common to the students' ImPACT projects and their other classroom activities. In this way, community-based organizations can be vehicles for both community activism and constructive school reform.

In closing, we want to stress that it is not enough in service programs to acknowledge that social problems exist. We need to go further to reflect on the sources of these problems and to build the skills and perspectives required for engaging in reform. There is value to service learning as a process that addresses needs and builds community, and there is another level on which the service experience can raise critical questions and open the door to social change. As Martin Luther King, Jr., observed, "Education without social action is a one-sided value because it has no potential; social action without education is a weak expression of energy." We think service learning provides an opportunity to integrate education and social action into a reciprocally intertwined, broad, and powerful whole. In this view service is not only a vehicle for substantive individual development and curricular enhancement; it is also an important foundation and springboard for social reform.

Notes

1. Jeff Claus was the initial director and Curtis Ogden is current director of the Learning Web community service program. The Learning Web is a community agency that works closely with schools, other agencies, businesses, and adult volunteers to provide youth in the county, between the ages of 12 and 21, with program opportunities for individualized apprenticeships, group community service, and entrepreneurial experience. For more about the Learning Web, see Claus, 1994, and Hamilton, 1981.

2. Freire's view of the ideal developmental state is expressed in his concept of "integration," which, he explains, "results from the capacity to adapt oneself to reality *plus* the critical capacity to make choices and to transform that reality" (1973, 4).

3. We encourage readers to consult the work of Shor (1992) and Freire (1970, 1973) directly for detailed and substantive discussion of these ideas and much more. Also recommended is Bigelow et al. (1994).

4. *Get It Together*, produced by John L. Jackson, Jr., and Melissa Brockett, 1993, available from The Video Project, 5332 College Avenue, Suite 101, Oakland, CA, 94618.

5. Two quotes we often use to generate discussion/reflection here are: "We make a living by what we get, but we make a life by what we give" (Winston Churchill) and "Life's most persistent and urgent question is what are you doing for others" (Martin Luther King, Jr.).

6. Books that are helpful in understanding and teaching the perspective and methods of anthropological/ethnographic research include James Spradley and David McCurdy's *The Cultural Experience: Ethnography in Complex Society*, 1972 (first edition) and 1996 (second edition), published by Science Research Associates; David Fetterman's *Ethnography: Step by Step*, 1989, published by Sage; and Ernest Stringer's *Community-Based Ethnography: Breaking Traditional Boundaries of Research, Teaching, and Learning*, 1997, published by Lawrence Erlbaum.

References

Banks, J. 1991. A curriculum for empowerment, action, and change. In C. Sleeter (Ed.), *Empowerment through multicultural education*. Albany, N.Y.: SUNY Press.

Beyer, L. 1996. Introduction: The meanings of critical teacher preparation. In L. Beyer (Ed.), *Creating democratic classrooms: The struggle to integrate theory and practice*. New York: Teachers College Press.

Bigelow, B., L. Christensen, S. Karp, B. Miner, and B. Peterson. 1994. Creating classrooms for equity and social justice. In B. Bigelow, L. Christensen, S. Karp, B. Miner, and B. Peterson (Eds.), *Rethinking our classrooms: Teaching for equity and justice*. Milwaukee, Wis.: Rethinking Our Schools.

Boyte, H. 1991. Community service and civic education. *Phi Delta Kappan*, 72: 765–767.

Bruner, J. 1996. *The culture of education*. Cambridge, Mass.: Harvard University Press.

Claus, J. 1994. The Learning Web: A grassroots, community-based model for youth apprenticeship. Paper presented at the annual meeting of the American Educational Research Association, New Orleans.

Freire, P. 1970. *Pedagogy of the oppressed*. New York: Seabury.

———. 1973. *Education for critical consciousness*. New York: Seabury.

———. 1992. Book jacket, back cover. In I. Shor, *Empowering education: Critical teaching for social change*. Chicago: University of Chicago Press.

Hamilton, S. 1981. The Learning Web: The structure of freedom. *Phi Delta Kappan*, 62, 600–601.

Jones, B., R. Maloy, and C. Steen. 1996. Learning through community service is political. *Equity and Excellence in Education*, 29(2): 37–45.

Kahne, J., and J. Westheimer. 1996. In the service of what? The politics of service learning. *Phi Delta Kappan*, 77: 593–599.

Karp, S. 1997. Educating for a civil society: The core issue is inequality. *Educational Leadership*, 54: 40–43.

Lakes, R. 1996. *Youth development and critical education: The promise of democratic action*. Albany, N.Y.: SUNY Press.

Ogden, C., and J. Claus. 1997. Reflection as a natural element of service: Service learning for youth empowerment. *Equity and Excellence in Education*, 30(1): 72–81.

Shor, I. 1992. *Empowering education: Critical teaching for social change.* Chicago: University of Chicago Press.

Sorensen, K. 1996. Creating a democratic classroom: Empowering students within and outside school walls. In L. Beyer (Ed.), *Creating democratic classrooms: The struggle to integrate theory and practice.* New York: Teachers College Press.

Youniss, J., and M. Yates. 1997. *Community service and social responsibility in youth.* Chicago: University of Chicago Press.

Chapter 6

Taking a Calculated Risk: Harnessing the Exuberance of Youth through "Community Problem Solvers"

Alice L. Halsted

On a suffocating day in August, I approached the community center in Forest Hills, New York, buoyed, despite the oppressive heat, by the favorable impression the young community activists had made the previous day on a VIP I had brought to meet with them. The Mountain Climbers, as they had named themselves, spoke with unrehearsed passion about what it meant to them to have been given the opportunity to be involved in their community. The heartfelt comments of a group that had coalesced after only six weeks of working together were gratifying indeed. One often wonders if kids are listening to all the messages we adults are trying to send. So to have heard these young people relate their pride and sense of accomplishment to a third party made me feel that the Community Problem Solvers process was working.

I saw many members of the group gathered near a large sprinkler set up in the playground. They dashed through the jets of water with the unself-consciousness of young children. I waved gaily, delighted to be back among them for a carefully planned afternoon of work on our project. To my disbelief, they ignored me. When I tried to get the group to gather, they told me, in effect, to get lost! The articulateness of the day before had evaporated; in its place was the attitude of today. Lesson One: Involving young people, especially young adolescents, in the process of social change can be an uneven experience. Some days are uplifting, and others are crushing. Lessons that one assumes have been indelibly conveyed are seemingly forgotten in the blink of an eye. But through the ups and downs of the process, I saw glimmers of maturity in these budding community activists. Through their work, the Mountain Climbers presaged an image of the contributing citizens these promising yet untested young people could become.

Engaging young people in the quest for societal change is a difficult and demanding task. One must be comfortable with the unpredictable nature of the process. As one social studies teacher put it, "When we began investigating our neighborhood, I did not know where our questions might lead." Yet it is just this sense of discovery that makes the work compelling. And when young people sense that their actions can change conditions in their community, they derive a sense of purpose and commitment that engenders hope for all involved.

Adolescents and Social Action

As they mature, young adolescents develop an understanding of abstract concepts such as *justice* and *the common good* that extend beyond their own self-absorption. This budding comprehension of and interest in social concerns must be nurtured for it to be lasting. Early adolescence is an opportune time to link young people to local institutions where they can turn their nascent interests into concrete action for the public good.

Whereas early in the century young people had a clearly defined place in the social order, the creation of the nuclear family and the acceleration of the pace of life has eroded opportunities for young adolescents to find their place in the world (Schine, 1989). But instead of pining for an idealized past that probably never existed, John Gardner exhorts us to "reinvent community":

> Out of deeply held values comes the sense of purpose and commitment that gives meaning to life. Humans long for meaning, and the first weaving of the web of meaning begins in the cradle and continues in the family, school, church, and neighborhood. . . . The traditional community, whatever its shortcomings, did create . . . a structure of social interdependency in which individuals gave and received support—all giving, all receiving. With that no longer available, *we must seek to reconstruct comparable systems of dependable interdependency wherever we can*—in the workplace, the church, the school, the youth-serving organizations, and so on. (italics added; 1992, 4)

Involvement in community issues offers young people a chance to test themselves in new roles, to learn how to contribute in constructive ways to the democratic process, and to discover a place for themselves in the world, thereby creating for themselves a vision of a personal future. Linking young people to adults in constructive roles represents an approach that can accomplish what Gardner seeks. But a tenuous sense of self, coupled with fluctuating feelings of inadequacy, makes early adolescence a particularly tender time. Involving young people ages 10–14 in community issues has its risks. Though involvement in addressing a social issue can be a transforming experience, it can just as easily heighten feelings of frustration and alienation. Success is not assured, and individual growth often comes slowly.

It is because of the risk involved in introducing the talents of an unpredictable group into the uncertainty of community work that the National Helpers Network created the Community Problem Solvers model (see National Helpers Network, 1996). For all the skills and experience one can acquire through community involvement, one can also create premature disillusionment in youth that might be difficult to overcome because of the vulnerability of adolescence. Although adults cannot shield young people from disappointment, we can prepare them to persevere in the face of difficulties and help them learn from these difficulties.

Educators are being urged to break down the walls between school and community and to allow young people to apply their skills and talents to community needs. Initiatives have appeared at all levels of government, especially at the federal level through the National and Community Service Act of 1990 and the Clinton administration's National Service Trust Act of 1993 to support community service and service learning. Linking young people through service to their communities has been promoted to support a variety of goals, from school reform to character development. Experts in youth development assert that young people involved in environmental action or community health campaigns will be seen as resources rather than drains on communities. Teachers and administrators have discovered how service can enliven curriculum. There is also broad agreement that for young people to achieve the learning and personal growth possible from community involvement, substantial planning must occur.

At the National Helpers Network, we have seen firsthand that young adolescents want to assume responsibility but need a clearly defined, realistic framework for their activities. They are looking for opportunities to test new skills and to prove to themselves, their peers, and the adults in their lives that they are competent, but they also want concrete goals and consistent structure. They want to test themselves in new settings, but they need to be able to retreat to a safe place where their observations and performance can be discussed in a caring atmosphere. A process is needed to meet the needs of young adolescents while simultaneously capitalizing on their talents. This is what we set out to do in creating Community Problem Solvers.

The Process Revealed

Community Problem Solvers combines structure with flexibility. Over a defined period, sometimes as short as six weeks, young people are guided to become effective teams through which each person's talents are valued and employed. The process is broken down into clearly defined, discrete elements that yield concrete results. *Concrete* is the operative word. Young people are introduced to the underlying concept that challenges, though demanding, can be approached in small steps. Breaking down big jobs into small pieces fills two functions: first, young people are made aware of the need for planning before execution; and second, they can see, literally, the fruits of their efforts in real ways.

It should be emphasized that Community Problem Solvers works equally well in schools and community-based agencies. The fundamental requirements for the process to work are the attention of a willing adult facilitator who believes in the capacity of young people to perform at high levels and the setting aside of a block of time, six weeks minimum, during which the same group of youngsters is able to meet together at regular intervals. The adult role is to guide young people to come to decisions fairly with the assurance that everyone's voice is heard in the decision-making process and to help young people persevere in executing the plan.

In the school setting, the organizing mechanism can be a class or a group of classes. Students at Cedar Heights Junior High School in Kent, Washington, collaborated across many different disciplines to restore an abandoned mining town in nearby Franklin. What began as a project in the social studies class burgeoned into a school collaboration as different skills were required to learn the history of the town, obtain the permits needed to restore some of its elements, and conduct the restoration. Students have mapped the site, conducted a full-scale archeological dig, and produced oral histories featuring interviews with community elders who remember the town. They have placed interpretive signs at the site, restored the coal cart, and beautified the cemetery. To help others learn more about the town, the students have written a play and produced a video and a book about Franklin. They also lead tours of the site for the entire school and teach lessons they developed themselves on Washington State history. A long-term goal for students was to qualify the town for the National Register of Historic Places, which they achieved. At a certain point, however, they realized that to continue the restoration work required skills that they did not possess. At this writing, the junior high school students have realized that they have contributed what they were able to bring Franklin back to life. Recognizing that construction would be required to perform the restoration of the main street, the students passed the project along to Kent's high school, where older students will apprentice at the site.

This is one example of the richness that can be derived from community involvement. But the attitude of Mike Papritz, the history teacher who guided the students, was crucial. He is comfortable with the open-ended nature of community action. He told me, "It's a challenge to be a teacher in an informal setting and not have all of the answers. That's my livelihood—where I don't have all the answers and I have to dig in with the kids to find the answers."

At the National Helpers Network, we wanted to aid other educators and youth workers who shared an interest in working with students on community issues by providing them with a structure that exploited the talents of their students while simultaneously addressing their needs. I like to think of the Solvers process as a structure around which teachers can shape a project. Woven throughout the project is a reflective component, critical to the service-learning experience, which enables young people to examine their progress and make sense of the experience.

The process is divided into the following steps:

1. Fostering Collaboration
2. Learning about Community
3. Choosing a Problem
4. Creating a Plan of Action
5. Implementing the Plan
6. Reflecting (embedded in all of the above)
7. Celebrating to Honor the Group's Accomplishments

Fostering Collaboration

In preparation for their introduction to community issues, Solvers (i.e., the young people in the program) first need to develop skills for working together effectively. They need to see the power that derives from group versus individual efforts. And especially among young adolescents, the groundwork for cooperation and collegiality must be laid in concrete ways.

This necessity of fostering group trust and collaboration may be the most difficult thing an adult facilitator is called on to do in the Community Problem Solvers process. Encouraging the Solvers to respect one another's opinions and observations, to observe rules about speaking in turn, and to understand the role of the adult in the process, all without undermining the ultimate responsibility that the young people hold in the process, requires skill and dedication. But it is critical to the integrity of the process and the ease with which the group operates for the period of the project.

First, Solvers must agree on the rules that will govern their meetings. The adult guides the young people in their decision making but must feel comfortable *not* making the decisions *for* them. The early sessions provide the group with an overview of what they can expect from the program. A discussion about deadlines and a timetable for the course of the project takes place, and rules of order and expectations are established for both the students and the adult facilitator.

I found it useful for my group to develop a mission statement and letter of commitment that they all signed. This document, in which they promised to do their best and support each other, grew in importance as I referred to it on the many occasions when their resolve was tested. At one point in the process, when interest was waning because we weren't succeeding in obtaining the permissions we needed to continue on our planned course of action, we agreed to draft a second letter of commitment. Solvers were given an opportunity to opt out of the work, but their signature on the second document meant that they were in it for the long haul. (After a particularly rich reflection seminar on the meaning of setting one's signature on a piece of paper, to my great relief, everyone signed.)

Solvers come to understand that a variety of talents are needed to complete a multifaceted project, and they develop skills essential for cooperation and problem solving. Through group-building activities, such as the creation of a group resumé, young people are given an opportunity to see how much they offer the community. Creative talents are called on when students decide on a name for the group, create a logo, and write a sample "want ad" to advertise their availability and skills. With these tools in hand, Solvers will be ready to market their services to the community.

Learning about Community

In this phase of the program, Community Problem Solvers perform an assessment of community needs to help them develop a realistic picture of pressing problems that exist and the resources available to address them. Solvers conduct surveys of the community, go on a scavenger hunt, visit local agencies, business, and public spaces, interview "people in the know," and compile a list of resources they discover to address problems.

Conducting the needs assessment helps Solvers achieve many different objectives. The study helps them:

- gain essential information they need to select their problem and complete the project
- develop and strengthen important research skills and gain a new level of confidence in gathering information from various sources, including publications, organizations, and individuals
- establish an important connection to the resources available in their communities

In addition to the tasks performed in the community, Solvers are helped to hone the skills they will need to collect essential information—skills in observation, interviewing, note taking, and telephone etiquette. With each new area treated, youngsters can make the connection between a required skill and its application in the real world.

Choosing a Problem

Armed with the facts obtained in their community investigations, Solvers are ready to analyze the information objectively. Activities for this segment enable Solvers to take a closer look at the problems they have identified, determine the advantages and disadvantages of selecting each, rank these issues in importance to the group, and, ultimately, narrow their choices to select one specific problem on which to work.

If Solvers are going to feel a genuine sense of ownership of their project, they should be allowed to direct the process of selection themselves. The adult facilitator offers guidance but refrains from inserting personal biases or preferences into the discussion. Throughout the process, however, the adult facilitator helps Solvers refine their arguments and steers them toward realistic goals. For example, if Solvers choose to address the issue of homelessness, the adult facilitator might point out options: students could offer help to individual homeless persons or collect food for a local shelter. Either option is more realistic than deciding to eradicate homelessness in the community.

Creating a Plan of Action

Once Solvers have decided on a problem to tackle, they will have to translate their idealism and their broad ideas into a concrete, detailed strategy. This can be a difficult task for young adolescents. It's one thing to say, "Let's do something about litter in our neighborhood"; it's quite another to outline exactly how to do that. Students will need the help of the adult facilitator as they make this critical leap from the general to the specific.

In this segment of the process, Solvers identify and prioritize specific goals and action steps for their project and establish a realistic timetable for accomplishing these goals. They will draw on the knowledge and skills they have gained in their training to identify specific objectives they must accomplish and to determine which of the many community resources they have learned about will be most useful to them.

For example, if Solvers choose to clean up the block surrounding their school or center, they may recall from one of their interviews that the Department of Sanitation provides bags and brooms for community service projects. When Solvers get down to devising their plans, they will realize that the community study was just as useful for identifying resources as it was for identifying problems. The importance of the group-building and problem-solving exercises performed earlier in the process will become especially apparent at this point, as Solvers develop a cohesive strategy and determine who will be responsible for specific tasks.

After Solvers have created their plan of action and settled on a timetable, it is important to emphasize what a milestone they have reached. They have learned to work together effectively. They have devised an equitable process for agreeing on a problem to be tackled. They have done research and identified resources. What might have seemed at the outset to be a difficult undertaking has become a clear plan.

Implementing the Plan

Solvers use the group collaboration, problem-solving, and critical-thinking skills they have developed to tackle the problem they have selected. The value of all the preparation in team building and group dynamics will become apparent as young Solvers perform their assigned tasks, confront obstacles, adjust their priorities, and move ahead.

In testing this model, we have been struck by the limitless possibilities for change that youth can effect, when given the proper guidance:

- Concerned about increasing gang violence in their community, Solvers wrote an original play exposing the dangers of gang membership and then performed it for younger girls at the camp to discourage them from becoming gang members.
- Solvers pitched in to clean up a local park, removing litter and painting over graffiti. They then created public service announcements and colorful posters to encourage the community to take better care of its parks and collected signatures on petitions asking the police to step up their park patrols.
- Solvers were dissatisfied with the appearance of the street on which their youth center was located, so they teamed up to brighten up a vacant lot, clearing it of litter and planting flowers and shrubs. They returned to the lot throughout the summer to care for their new garden. In the process of restoring the flower beds on their street, they learned about a home for emotionally troubled adults located near the community center. It happened that Solvers shared misperceptions about the purpose of the residence with other community members, assuming that it was a residence for the elderly. Not knowing the real purpose of the center, local citizens believed that the staff of the institution treated the residents unkindly. Once the Solvers made contact with the director of the center, they were able to inform neighbors of the challenges the caregivers faced in helping the adults who resided there.

Reflecting (Embedded in All of the Above)

Growth and learning are not automatic consequences of participation in a service experience but result from a young person's deliberate efforts to make sense of the experience, to learn from it, and to act on the insights gained. One of the challenging but rewarding aspects of the adult facilitator will be to help the Solvers learn how to reflect on their experiences throughout the process. Analyzing situations in a critical manner, articulating feelings and reactions, placing events in context, moving beyond the specific experience and identifying the broader issues involved—all these are extremely valuable skills for young adolescents. Reflection helps them to think about their world and about themselves, and these skills are transferable to other learning situations.

It has been my experience that some of the richest reflection sessions spring from difficult experiences. The Mountain Climbers' quixotic temperaments preordained periodic outbursts of anger and frustration when plans didn't proceed in a seamless fashion. Sometimes conflict arose from setbacks such as running into an exceptionally brusque receptionist at a local agency. Other times, internecine rivalries threatened to sink the effort.

These flare-ups became the subject of our most interesting reflection sessions, where we talked freely but respectfully about the challenges we had promised to overcome in order to contribute to community life. (The Solvers had established rules of order for these sessions during the "fostering collaboration" segment of the process.) Suggestions were offered on how to negotiate the bureaucracy and how to deal with personal differences of opinion. I cannot state that all the youngsters became fast friends as a result of their participation, but I can say that they were able to put differences aside and work together. Recognizing that Mountain Climbers were all newcomers to the United States—from Bangladesh to Rwanda, from the Philippines to Colombia—this was no small thing.

Celebrating to Honor the Group's Accomplishments

One of the most striking lessons for me was the realization that the Mountain Climbers needed to have their achievements pointed out to them to realize that they had accomplished something. The Standards for School-Based Service Learning adopted by the Alliance for Service Learning in Education Reform emphasize the importance of recognition:

> In large and small ways during the period of service as well as with a culminating event, students should share with the community and their peers what has been gained and given through service. . . . In a society that values work and measures people's importance by the jobs that they do, young people, especially adolescents, are perceived as non-contributing members of the society. Credit for their achievements, affirmation of the skills they have mastered, and appreciation for the time they have devoted to the community should be acknowledged publicly. (ASLER, 1993, 7)

These recognition events can take the form of informal parties or formal ceremonies. They need not be costly or elaborate. Simply setting aside some time for young people to gather with their adult collaborators to reflect on their accomplishments and feel a sense of shared pride "reinforces the significance of the enterprise and the worth of the young people" (ASLER, 1993, 7).

Gardner states, "The healthy community has many ways of saying to the individual, 'You belong, you have a role to play, and the drama has meaning'" (1992, 6). People need to hear that message as adolescents perhaps more than at any other time of their lives. With a primary function of community being to provide identity and a sense of belonging, celebratory gatherings take on higher meanings. They not only provide pleasurable moments, but they also reinforce the critical message that young people need to hear—the message that they matter, that their lives have worth, and that the community needs them.

The Contract

For the Problem Solvers program to work, there must be a clear agreement between the adult facilitator and the young people that it is the young people who will decide on the issue to be addressed. The facilitator must be comfortable with the role of guide rather than leader, stepping in when needed to shift course when the group is floundering or to remind young people of their responsibility to stay on course. A collegial atmosphere in which trust exists between the group and the adult facilitator yields the most fruitful results. In the volatile world of adolescence, the adult can provide the ballast for the shifting opinions and strong feelings of the team.

The adult cannot lead in the traditional sense of laying out the tasks and setting the agenda. I admit that this was a difficult hurdle for me to cross in my experience with Solvers. As I became aware of the needs of the community that we researched together, I was convinced that the investigation of traffic accidents on a local highway would be a superb project to involve the teens, exposing them to many different types of information and testing their skills and reasoning ability. But this option did not appeal to them at all. Although it was difficult, I was forced by our agreement to abandon my interests and yield to the wisdom of the group. I don't regret it.

In the end, the Mountain Climbers wanted to perform a cleanup in a local playground that they frequented after school. It became clear to me that this play area was very important to them and to their siblings. Their vested interest in a safe place to play motivated them to obtain permits and equipment from the Parks Department to clean up the space and write and perform a play for local residents to encourage their cooperation in maintaining it. All this was done during only part of a summer by young people who did not know each other at the outset and who possessed markedly different skill levels.

Despite our ups and downs, we all came away with a sense of accomplishment. The administrators at the community house were so pleased with our work that they consulted the young people for opinions on a grant proposal they were preparing. The young people were astonished at this opportunity, stunned that adults would ask their viewpoint on such a weighty matter. For a brief moment, the lines of demarcation between the generations blurred as the groups consulted with each other on plans that would affect both in the year to come.

Conclusion

Dr. René Bendit of the German Youth Institute in Munich describes adult attitudes toward youth as falling into two categories (1997). His research documents one group of adults who believe young people embody our hopes for the future and another who believe young people pose a threat to society because of their destructive behavior. I fall, unabashedly, into the former camp, not, I believe, out of a sense of misguided optimism but because young people have proven their abilities to me countless times through their service in programs across the country.

I have met with thousands of young adolescents who have served their communities in myriad ways. I have copresented with them at workshops and collaborated with them on student-run program evaluations. What I have consistently found is that regardless of their performance in school, they are interested in and capable of making substantial contributions to their communities and the well-being of others. In fact, it is often those youth who are the most "challenging" in the classroom who are the most involved and effective in the real world work of service and problem solving.

It is precisely because of the hopes young people have shared with me and because of their sense of yearning for a chance to test themselves in the world of adults that the Community Problem Solvers process was created. My time with the Mountain Climbers came and went too quickly before they were off to pursue the next chapter in their busy lives. But in that short time, we coalesced as a group, named ourselves, created a motto and a logo, performed a community needs assessment, visited local service providers (from the Community Planning Board to the neighboring fire station), agreed on an issue to address, developed and carried out a plan, performed a park cleanup, and publicized our efforts in the writing of an original play that was performed for parents, friends, and neighbors. We suffered setbacks along the way, but nothing severe enough to prevent us from carrying out our plan. And along the way we developed respect for one another and the different talents individuals brought to the group. Not bad for seven weeks of work!

Unleashing young people into the community has its risks, but with a clear structure in place success can be built at each stage, and the risk of failure, while not eliminated, can be managed. In the process, the resources, talents, and sheer enthusiasm of young people can be applied to achieving a better future for us all.

References

ASLER (Alliance for Service Learning in Education Reform). 1993. *Standards for school-based service learning.* New York.

Bendit, R. 1997. From remarks made at the International Seminar on Education and Community Service. Buenos Aires, Argentina. July 2, 1997.

Gardner, J. 1992. *Reinventing community.* New York: Carnegie Foundation.

National Helpers Network. 1996. *Community problem solvers: youth leading change.* New York: National Helpers Network.

Schine, J. 1989. *Young adolescents and service learning.* New York: Carnegie Foundation.

Chapter 7

What's Love Got to Do With It?: Teen Dancers on Community Service Learning

Tricia Bowers-Young and Richard D. Lakes

This chapter will profile five members of the Apprentice Corporation, a teen performance company at Moving in the Spirit (MITS), an alternative community-based, service-learning group that uses dance as a vehicle for teaching youth the values of discipline, respect, accountability, responsibility, and commitment. The teen dancers "work" in a model program with an incentive system that rewards them with daily points for successful participation in a variety of service-learning activities, including peer teaching in a pregnancy prevention program. Apprentice Corporation youth use the incentive system as a way to earn 1,200 "MITS dollars," the purchase cost for joining the summer road tour which involves performing at various sites around the country. Any remaining "dollars" earned by the students are used to "purchase" donated items of clothing, toys, jewelry, and electronics in the MITS Christmas store. The teens are issued checking accounts for over-the-counter transactions, which gives them some experience in money management.

Apprentice Corporation teens are a multiracial, multiethnic, and gender-mixed group of inner-city youths, ages 12 to 19, who perform in public spaces in the city as well as in summer venues throughout the nation and abroad. Membership is by yearly audition, and participants take classes in dance technique free of charge. The program fulfills the 75 hours of voluntary service required by the Atlanta Public Schools.

Social justice themes are represented in the choreographic presentations of this urban ensemble. For example, *Force* addresses the absurdity of violence; *Pressure* deals with the stark statistics of teenage pregnancy; *Behind Dark Glasses* speaks to self-esteem and the painful road to healing; and *Freedom* promotes racial reconciliation. We will profile dancers involved in the Apprentice Corporation from May to August 1997, featuring their viewpoints on community service that utilizes dance performance for peer education.[1] We will also highlight the personal reflections of the youth as they grew into adolescent leaders and the reflections of parents regarding the influence of the program on their child's development.

Perhaps an endorsement of community service learning is captured best by the words of Elaine, a recent high school graduate who spoke openly in the pages of a youth-run newspaper about crossing borders to advance racial reconciliation. She said:

> One thing I noticed when I joined the Apprentice Corporation is that by being white, I was in the minority. This didn't bother me, however, as most of my experiences at school and at the Girl's Club were similar. In fact, this only heightened my experiences at Moving in the Spirit. I learned there that you have something in common with almost everyone you meet and that economic and racial barriers tend to crumble as you begin to know and trust someone. (Maynard, 1997, 14)

We believe that Elaine, like others in her cohort of today's activist youth, will keep the civic imperative alive, generating renewed focus and energy toward community commitment and neighborhood renewal.

Kathy

Kathy, 20, first became involved in MITS when she was a nine-year-old at the local Girl's Club and has been with the program ever since—11 years. She lives at home with her mother, currently unemployed, and her father, who is disabled. Kathy graduated from high school in 1995, attends a local community college studying physical therapy, and works part-time as an administrative intern and a dance teacher with MITS. We asked Kathy what she liked most about the program: "I like when we dance. And I like how it takes up a lot of our time, like when I was younger, I didn't have too much to do, so it took up a lot of my time and kept my mind occupied. And I like what it stands for. They try to incorporate that into your everyday living, and they use dance classes to try to practice respect and responsibility, commitment and accountability in your everyday life."

Interestingly, when Kathy talked about the powerful influences of her dance program she noted that it provided the discipline needed to control one's negative behaviors, what she termed "attitude." "We had to leave our attitude outside," she remarked about the instructional setting. She also recognized the transferability of positive attitude beyond the classroom, at work and with peers. There are consequences for negative actions in life, Kathy said, such as not calling an employer when you are going to be late.

"I've learned to talk to people and tell people my feelings instead of holding them in." She credited MITS with developing self-awareness and emotional maturity, in part because she realized that the Apprentice Corporation provided regular opportunities for her to release tension and stress through engaging in physical activity, as well as being part of a social community of teen dancers. More important, her non-MITS friends were unable to benefit from the creative energy she experienced on a regular basis. They were not connected to social action through community service; they were alienated, bored, and anomic. She discerned:

> When they don't have anything to do, they're either upset, or their mind is idle. And they'll end up depressed or either mad at everything. And if I call them . . . they're either mad or frustrated or depressed. So I can tell a difference. Just not having anything to do as a whole, they end up getting into a lot of trouble, fights, etc. Not saying that it's a pattern or anything, but pregnancy, drugs, and stuff. I've learned with MITS that I can make choices of my own, and I don't have to follow the crowd or anything.

Perhaps the most insightful comments Kathy offered were about the emotional states of her friends, recognizing their varying degrees of melancholy. "I can look at some my friends now, and some of my friends are not happy. And I can just tell it by their conversations, and I can tell by the way they are looking and stuff." She perceived that they were "in denial," unable to voice their concerns and make connections with others. "Communication is the key to a lot of stuff," Kathy remarked to one friend; if "you communicate your feelings to that person, then they will know how to talk to you and how to treat you the next time when you are in the same situation."

Kathy has learned about multicultural community as well. She attributes the dance company specifically with helping her to accept diversity and reach a level of tolerance for differences. "It's like, if I wasn't with MITS I wouldn't be too open and stuff. I wouldn't." The

variety of people and places she has visited in performances throughout the city and elsewhere have brought her in contact with audience
members from all walks of life. In addition, Kathy has participated in
MITS-sponsored peer workshops on tolerance, training students in
valuing diversity. (She served as a peer mediator when conflicts arose
at Apprentice Corporation and at her high school.) Peer teachings
gave her an opportunity to help instill in students a set of workplace
values that could translate into other areas of life.

Chris

Chris, 18, first became involved in MITS while attending a neighborhood Boy's and Girl's Club. At age 12 she auditioned for the Apprentice Corporation and has been a member ever since. She lives with
her mother, a computer specialist, and her father, a minister. Chris
graduated from high school in 1997 and attends college in the East,
majoring in modern dance. She was an administrative intern with MITS
and spokesperson for their peer education pregnancy prevention program. When asked how Moving in the Spirit affected her life, she said:
"Man, I would be a totally different person [without MITS]. And probably wouldn't even be aware of who I am, or feelings that I have, like
emotions. Or why I do the things I do, or feel a certain way. And then
I wouldn't have had the element of dance, of expressing myself, getting those emotions out."

Her involvement in the creative aspects of making dances provoked
a strong response. Like most participants in the ensemble, Chris benefited from learning how to channel the psychic energy and physical
growth of childhood into performance. The MITS dance classes she
had at age 10, she said, "added a lot of grace" at that very awkward
age; later, she benefited from more sophisticated technical instruction
as well as from opportunities to build confidence when performing on
stage. In the beginning, however, Chris thought of herself as "the
typical white girl," "very sheltered," who "didn't have any rhythm."
But over time she learned how to dance, to teach combinations to her
friends, to construct new choreography, to participate in ensemble
work, and to experiment with a variety of musical styles.

Through membership in the Apprentice Corporation Chris was given
opportunities for closeness and connection with teens in a safe environment—a trusting place where "you can learn about people."[2] In
fact, Chris revealed that she didn't like school because of the negative

aspects of socializing, cliques that create barriers and divisions among people who are "putting on a front at school." On the other hand, MITS is a youth organization where one finds authentic, genuine engagement with peers who communicate openly and honestly. As a result, Chris views MITS as a kind of sanctuary:

> I like to be here as much as I possibly can. So a lot of times if we don't have school, or if we have a day off of school or something I come here. Or, if I have nothing to do then I'll come here to help or to hang out or take a break from school. See, I really don't get much out of school, and I'd rather be here, and I feel more productive here. . . . School just drags on, so I look forward to coming here. And when I go home, I'm like, I'd rather be here.

Although Chris had difficulty motivating herself in academic work (even though she maintained an excellent grade-point average), she found dance activity to be fun, challenging, and exciting. Not to be downplayed in this discussion of Chris's maturation are the career development insights gained from her part-time work as an administrative intern at Moving in the Spirit. That is, Chris spoke about the type of caring workplace she envisioned, modeled along the lines of her present place of employment. She explained: "Even now when I think about getting a job, and I hear people talk about, 'Oh, I'm working here as a cashier.' I think, isn't that boring just standing all day, and you don't make any progress. Oh, yeah, 'I checked out 35 people today.' I think 'NO!' I like to make progress. I like to make people feel good. It's like MITS has offered the creative aspect to work."

Chris told us how much personal autonomy she felt when working there. At first, MITS was just a place for her "to hang" after school. But then her emotional investment grew to the point where she was volunteering to assist the office staff with simple clerical duties. Now her formal job description has been upgraded to grant writing as well as editing the monthly newsletter. And she had been given more responsibility at work, especially as a spokesperson in the area of public relations. Chris is also the sole student representative to the organization's board of directors and was the coordinator of fundraising for the European tour.

The opportunities for teen empowerment through work at community service agencies should be cultivated and encouraged, not dismissed. Students like Chris can be valuable assets in the maintenance and sustainability of youth organizations. Young people can assume positions of responsibility and leadership through inclusion in organi-

zational affairs. Aside from the vocational aspects of learning workplace skills and competencies, however, teens derive additional value
from mentorship in positive lifestyles while cultivating peer friend-
ships.[3] Chris now knows that she wants a work setting that values
human relationships, that abides by the three Cs—caring, connection,
and community. After college graduation, she told us, she might come
back to work at MITS or maybe create another nonprofit organization. Through peer education projects at MITS, moreover, she realized that teaching may be a future occupational prospect. "It is such a
proud moment to watch the delight of your students," she said, "when
they feel accomplishment or are having fun."

Clarence

Clarence, 19, lives with his mother, who is disabled from an auto
accident (his father is deceased). He first saw the Apprentice Corporation perform at age 11, auditioned for the ensemble the next year,
and has been a member ever since. He graduated from high school in
1997 and attends college in town.

When we asked Clarence to tell us how MITS changed his life, he
volunteered, "MITS has taught me a lot about how to talk to people
and how to treat people. And it has taught me that no matter what
color a person is they can always receive a fair chance at anything."
Most important, Clarence confirmed that MITS indeed was a safe haven from the cruel and mean-spirited city. In fact, Chris's metaphor of
sanctuary within a caring youth organization reappears again and again
in Clarence's words, "Everytime I came here it has always been a
loving attitude. And that's a good thing, because today's world is hard
and love is kind of hard to find in a harsh world. I come here and I feel
like I'm on another planet."

Clarence also credited his personal success to the peer education
activities of MITS pregnancy prevention workshops, a community
service project funded by the March of Dimes. He learned to hone
public speaking skills, gain confidence in fielding questions from an
audience, and reaffirm to others the workplace values he learned
through MITS. Clarence told us about the satisfactions he gained from
peer teaching: "I get a chance to do a lot of mentoring, and I get a
chance to give a lot of advice. And that's a good thing. I mean you
teach every day of your life."

Additionally, Clarence benefited from community service learning
projects that taught him, among other things, conflict resolution skills.

"I can talk my way out of a fight instead of actually engaging," he said. "Always go back to the values," he told us, "have the discipline to stay on track, have the accountability to know if you mess up it's okay." He continued: "Take it. Move on with your life. Learn from it, and don't do it again. I spread this knowledge all over—every time I get a chance to say something to a younger person, or someone that I know, my peers or whatever, I always spread the message. You've got to have the discipline, the accountability, and be responsible for your actions."

The dance performances within the pregnancy prevention workshops reaffirm the workplace values as well. For example, "Preconceptions" encourages teens to postpone sexual involvement, and "Pregnant Pause" illustrates the possible consequences of fly-by-night relationships.

One time we accompanied the Apprentice Corporation in an afterschool show at the Macon Youth Development Center (YDC), a juvenile justice facility for incarcerated girls in a remote area outside of the city. At the YDC, the company entertained more than 100 inmates (supervised by a handful of youth workers), about 90 percent of them African American, who had gathered together from six or seven residential cottages on the property. The performance lasted 45 minutes, with a 5-minute question-and-answer session afterward.

Several ensembles were memorable: a dance about the civil rights movement, one on teenage pregnancy, another symbolic of AIDS activism. The most popular piece, "Pregnant Pause," a duet featuring a male and a female member of the troupe, was performed as a romantic interlude accompanied by a recording of Frank Sinatra's "Strangers in the Night." The audience loved this number, asking many questions afterward about its meaning and creation. At the end of the program, as the inmates filed out of the assembly hall in groups based on cottage assignments, one of them remarked, "These kids are going to be somebody someday!"

Clarence is somebody, an amazing young man who has surfaced as a leader and model of success in this particular youth development organization. Despite the odds stacked against black male teens, however, Clarence overcame major threats to adolescent adjustment, including his mother's paralysis, his parents' divorce, his father's untimely death, and his being tracked in special education classes at school. The passing of his father as a result of alcoholism was particularly difficult for Clarence. "I wish there was a man in my family who could tell me the secrets of life," he said. Still, Clarence honors his father's memory with three little mementos: a piece of his father's blue workshirt, a scriptural passage, and the tissue he cried on at the funeral. "I saved them in a little black bag," he noted. He then recalled the following incident: "One day, during a track meet, I tied the bag to my shoes. When people asked me about it, I said, 'Your daddy is here, ain't he? Well, my daddy is here, too.' And when I came around the last curve, I felt like something was pushing me. I wasn't just running on my own energy anymore" (quoted in McCord, 1995, M3).

"Moving in the Spirit always kept that loving environment," Clarence said once again; it "always kept on giving encouragement to my mom and me." Clarence reminisced about the time a program counselor provided guidance and support when he was feeling low, after his grandfather died. He said:

> Tricia cried with me, for how long? Hours, it was a long time. And I started hollering out, "I ain't got nobody." Tricia always kept saying, "You've got me, you can come live with me. It's okay." And it brings me to tears now, just thinking about the times when I wasn't so on top of my game. How I had to adjust and just knowing that the values were there. And I could dig deep and get those values that were moving into me. That's something I can always, always go back to.

Clarence's wisdom certainly was derived from the values instilled in him at a tender age. Rather than fall off the precipice, as do so many children who are labeled at risk, Clarence directed his life with agency, power, control, and conviction.

Elaine

Elaine, 18, lived in Atlanta with her parents, who both work in the nonprofit field. She became involved with MITS at age eight, auditioned for the Apprentice Corporation four years later, and has been with the ensemble ever since. She graduated from high school in 1997 and attends a private college in Indiana. Elaine was spokesperson for the peer education pregnancy prevention series and a peer mediator. When asked a series of questions about her leadership development, specifically, if she would characterize herself as a leader, she promptly replied, "Sure." She then launched into a description of her behavior: "I'm a very talkative, loud person. I like to know exactly what's going on. Kind of a 'control thing.' So I tend to be more organized; I tend to organize people more than people organize me."

Elaine qualified this statement some, saying that since the Apprentice Corporation was based on a cohesive alliance of peers, she did her part in trying to maintain harmony and balance within the group. In fact, she knew that "allegiance and loyalty" were key factors in maintaining closeness and togetherness. Still, she said, "people will let stupid little misunderstandings get in the way." Perhaps she could best be described as a peacemaker, helping to forge unity while downplaying conflict among the teen dancers.

Elaine's experiences with peer training gave her some indication that a critically reflective education is important. For instance, she recognized that adolescents are more likely to make healthy decisions about life choices, such as having a baby, if properly informed by fellow peers about the consequences of teen pregnancy. "What we tell them [students] can have a big effect . . . make a big difference in their lives," she claimed. "So just the fact that I give somebody knowledge, then it empowers them to be in more control of what they are doing, to know more about what they are doing." Elaine cautioned that the teachings of social justice issues through choreography, however, may be too sophisticated for some teen audiences. She told about the time the group performed an antiwar number and some viewers were unable to understand the nuances of the piece. At other times the teen audiences "have an attitude" not very conducive to learning the movement themes.

Finally, Elaine shared with us her perspectives on personal growth through membership in the dance ensemble. She mentioned time and again that in a space where differences are respected, each teen can focus on clarifying his or her personal values. "It's made me realize more what I value," she remarked, "and how it's different maybe from what other people value." And the caring, loving environment at MITS nurtured the dancer's self-awareness, self-discipline, and agency. The ensemble "has made me a lot more responsible for what my actions are . . . not letting other people influence me in negative ways." She continued, "I'm letting myself know that I control my own actions . . . that it's my body and I can do whatever I want to."

Alisha

Alisha, 20, the youngest of four siblings, lived in Atlanta with her parents. She became involved with MITS at age nine through the neighborhood Boy's and Girl's Club. She was a member of Apprentice Corporation and a speaker with the peer education project as well. Alisha, a 1995 high school graduate, is in her third year at the University of Georgia.

When asked about her leadership abilities through MITS, she told us that they were at a "high level" because she participated in a number of related activities such as teaching dance, assisting with trainings, and working in the office, among others. Furthermore, she noted that her decision-making abilities helped gain recognition among her peers, who "admire that and view me as a leader. They constantly come to me for advice, and usually follow it." She added "I keep a positive attitude, and try to remember to treat people the way I want to be treated."

Finally, Alisha told us that she believes peer teachings can make a difference in other's lives, in particular because the dances are very relevant to the experiences of adolescents. Most teens can relate to MITS performances as "issues that concern them."

The Parents

We asked the parents of our interviewees a series of questions that illuminated the positive development of the teen dancers. All of the parents spoke highly of MITS and the Apprentice Corporation. Interestingly, we found that each of the parents had prepared their children to participate in community service projects primarily through church activities, serving the poor and homeless. Several of the teens and their parents participated in service-learning programs at school as well.

We asked a series of questions to elicit feedback on the strengths of each parent/child relationship. Alisha's mother remarked that she felt her daughter was "more trustworthy, more accountable" now. She reflected that her child had become "more responsible and dependable," with a visible increase in leadership skills development. She told us that Alisha had learned to appreciate diversity and respect differing attitudes. Finally, she said that MITS had kept her daughter "out of trouble" because it occupied quite a lot of her time. "Through MITS," she continued, Alisha was "able to help others—which is good."

Kathy's mother told us that MITS improved parent-child bonds: "We both have a more open mother/daughter relationship. We share our differences and problems with each other and pray about it." Apparently, Kathy was able to overcome her shyness in part because of the dance experiences; her mother said that now she could relate better to her siblings. "I have observed my daughter develop into a fine young lady, nice personality, and a positive outlook on life." She added that Kathy "likes to see people happy as well as being happy herself."

Most important, Kathy's adolescent development was enhanced by MITS's creation of a genuine community for the dancers. Her mother affirmed that the Apprentice Corporation was a place where her daughter found "people that care, love, and respect her for what she is. . . . They all watch over each other; they are a great family. When she is not home they are her family away from home."

Clarence's mother talked about how her son's involvement in MITS brought them together through dance. She attended performances with friends as well as organizational meetings (she is a member of the MITS community board). She even designed and constructed costumes for the troupe. Through all of these activities, she told us, "MITS serves as a common bond for my child and I."

She highlighted the travel and tour opportunities provided her son through Apprentice Corporation, and told us that in the past seven years he had been to more than 80 cities and performed for more than 130,000 people. Also, he recently toured abroad in Hungary and the Czech Republic. The dance company has "opened up many doors and opportunities" for Clarence, she stated. MITS is a "second home for my child."

Additionally, we were told that Clarence received many kudos for his service work with MITS. She had seen pictures of his dance performances posted on the school's bulletin board along with publicity releases for upcoming events or television spots. Some of the teachers gave the company personal donations as well. And, through his work with peer pregnancy prevention trainings, some of Clarence's classmates sought him out for advice about dating and birth control. She beamed: "He got positive leadership and guidance from MITS."

We were most intrigued with the words of Elaine's mother, who revealed to us that her child was difficult to raise, "a defiant streak in her which would try my patience." Elaine was destined for the storms and stresses of adolescence, we were told. "She would challenge rules and even break rules to make her point." Yet through MITS and dance, her teenage daughter grew in many positive, constructive ways—in fact, she turned out to be no trouble at all. The point is that Elaine gained self-confidence and self-esteem through modern dance, learning movements that helped her—tall and gangly for her age—develop grace and poise. Her mother attributes Elaine's newfound comfort with her body to dance experiences through MITS. "This self-confidence affects her relationships with peers, teachers, ministers, and everybody else."

Elaine had to work hard at dance, her mother said. Although excelling in academics at school, for instance, she was not as physically talented or athletic as some of her peers in the ensemble. Still, the community of dancers helped Elaine blossom as a group leader and company spokesperson. Her mother offered: "The experiences of personally knowing others of varied family configurations, family experiences, racial backgrounds, and economic status has made Elaine a better person. The challenges of touring and living with others day and night for extended periods of time have made her more aware of others' feelings and what it takes to get along."

Lastly, Chris's mother told us that her daughter learned much from the staff at MITS. The presence of a trained counselor, for instance, provided a positive adult mentor for the teens—very important in the case of Chris, who found someone she could turn to for advice and assistance. "It is very comforting to know that she has excellent adult role models," her mother said, "that she can look up to and ask questions of, that she may not feel comfortable talking with us about." We knew that Chris learned how to work successfully with adults; her communication skills facilitated intergenerational partnerships at MITS. And, her mother confirmed, Chris was able to "present a teenage view" to adults in the organization, which led to her "maturity and confidence around adults." "Not only does MITS provide a safe place for her to ask questions and get good advice," she continued, Chris "has gotten good factual information about sexuality, pregnancy prevention, STDs [sexually transmitted diseases], and dealing with peer pressure."

Teen Empowerment

A number of themes emerge from the voices of youths profiled at Moving in the Spirit. We see how young people join an organization that promotes mutuality, cooperation, commitment, and solidarity with service projects through the medium of dance. We are privy to the ways that these young people explore their self-identities in healthy, affirmative ways. We also recognize that they have access to learning about an ethic of love and caring for others—perhaps *the* major theme among these interviews. The Apprentice Corporation helps youths learn how to practice racial and ethnic reconciliations, gender affirmations, and interfaith harmonies. It provides opportunities for respecting cultural differences and learning tolerance and for examining structural barriers that limit growth. Authentic learning communities such as these allow participants safe places to share human needs, identify values, and deepen connections to their inner selves and to others.

Interestingly, the teen dancers we talked to articulated what may be the most important facet of community building in this particular arts venue—that is, closeness, in particular, physical and emotional contact through performance. Chris asked us to imagine how difficult it must be just to choreograph and direct adolescents. "Put 12 teenagers together," she said, "use this word and this word and take this text and lift each other. . . . Most people would not feel comfortable walking into a place and letting each other lift them." And, "with dance," she continued, you have to "really trust each other. And when you trust each other, you can learn about people, where they come from and stuff like that."

Dance breaks down those barriers to human connection. Elaine talked about the community of dancers as follows: "Being comfortable with all types of people is especially critical in dance because of the physical closeness involved. This closeness can also become emotional" (Maynard, 1997, 4). Clarence offered his gendered perspective on female dancers, what it is like traveling with them on tour and lifting and holding them in performances: "That alone is a learning experience. I've learned how to communicate with females, and how to adjust to their moods. Not to say that all have moods. And I'm learning that all don't have moods. But it's opened me up to a whole new world that I wasn't used to, or haven't been exposed to before that."

Kathy offered a very mature perspective about maintaining group harmony among the teens. She remarked that "by trying to control myself," she could help the group. That is, "I try to cooperate with people . . . just try to get along." She recognized that interpersonal relationships are difficult to maintain. Given the short amount of time some teens in the ensemble spend together, she wanted to "do her best to get along and make the situation better than what it could be." Chris added: "The way I interact with my friends is a result of the things I have learned from MITS. Because of the experiences of tours and living with diverse people, I make an effort to communicate with my friends and parents on many different levels."

We asked the dancers if they felt the performance themes were appropriate for teen audiences. Chris offered that the dances could

"reach this age group" since the company members were teens themselves, able to relate to their peers and make dances from their lived
experiences. Clarence added that the choreographic depictions of mock
violence portrayed on stage resonated with teen viewers. While the
dancers agreed that they were role models for their youthful audiences, they also recognized that young adults were better spectators
and more aware of the messages embedded in each piece. Alisha told
us that high school students were more capable of understanding social issues such as racism. "The older audiences, they see us, a mixed
group doing dances that relate to real issues," she said. "And they're
like, 'This is wonderful.' And, 'How are y'all doing this? I can't believe
this is real.' And, they kind of come at us like, 'Wow!'" Elaine recalled
that some audience members told her they were moved to tears over
certain dance numbers.

Conclusion

We have suggested that youth participation in community service
projects leads to healthy adolescent development.[4] Once empowered
with critical insights, young people can exhibit positive, real-life dis-
plays of their visions, dreams, and ambitions. In addition, youth organizations provide young people with a level of economic and political
self-determination and community control. While it is beyond the scope
of this chapter to document the varieties of self-help urban renewal
projects preparing youths for service,[5] we are mindful that grassroots
alliances and neighborhood coalitions enable teens to join with adults
in efforts that build both competence and community. Problematizing
and strategizing for community justice offers youths an opportunity to
have a voice in decisions that benefit them and their neighborhoods.
Teens are seen as important resources in local improvement efforts;
they are citizen-activists for community empowerment.

We have argued that youth empowerment is facilitated by a loving,
caring community of what Karen Pittman (1996) has termed "natural
actors"—the nexus of family, peers, neighbors, and community institutions surrounding a child's positive relationships to the environment.
"Programs and organizations do have an impact on youths' lives,"
Pittman observes, "but this impact is either amplified or dampened by
the quality and congruence of what else is going on in young people's
families, peer groups, and neighborhoods" (6–7). We are reminded of
Paulo Freire's dictum to practice what he terms "co-intentional educa-

tion," by which he means that liberatory knowledge and conscious-
ness-raising activities usher forth when leaders join with "the people"
to read the world and recognize it critically (Freire, 1995, 51). We can
think of at least five teen leaders who fit this model of empowerment,
because they offer their peers a Freirean-style critical education for
social justice.[6]

Certainly, these young people rejected the notion of volunteerism
as charitable acts oftentimes cloaked in lovelessness.[7] None of them
considered MITS to be structured in that way. Clarence said it was his
"mission" to have "people learn from it." In his words, he was driven
to "spread knowledge throughout the community" by offering popular
education through performance. Clarence and the other dancers are
waging a struggle for freedom—through the medium of dance—in which
they give voice to the reality of oppression and the lives of the oppressed. "We learn something from it [the project]," Chris remarked,
and we learn something "about others." But whether it is dance or
communication, she added, "we are just giving others an opportunity
to see into things." Elaine clarified: "MITS is more than you feel good
because you are helping somebody. You feel good because you are
helping yourself while you are helping other people." Still, the dancers view themselves as teen role models desiring to transform the
broken dreams and unfulfilled wishes of their peers. Alisha reflected:
"When kids see teenagers doing something else besides just hanging
around the house, just looking at TV or whatever, it kind of gives
them the feeling that 'I should do that,' or 'I want to do something
else.' Go the extra goal or whatnot." Clarence agreed: "We are making a difference. There are a lot of people out there that might be
feeling bad or down that day, and they come in this place, and they
see these kids dancing and having fun on the stage." Chris chimed in,
"Even if it's just keeping them off the street for an hour. You know. At
least we did something. It's not like we're out to save the world or
anything."

Finally, the dancers told us that they learned best when given opportunities to teach, as in the March of Dimes–funded pregnancy prevention workshops which provided a solid curriculum for extended
study and learning. For example, Elaine remembered the intense initial half-a-dozen training periods prior to actual workshop delivery,
where peer leaders talked about "what to expect and how to prepare.
. . .We went over the information we were going to have, and we just
brainstormed on how the audience would react." Clarence still regarded

the knowledge he received about birth control to be useful "lifelong—a lifetime message." Alisha remarked that knowing "accurate information" allows others to make more informed choices. Chris reflected on peer education at length: "I've learned a lot, more as the years go by. I mean we learned. Each performance we make an effort to learn more and more and read more information." Later, she offered: "Just being able to do statistics, you know, 'one out of every five girls,' and break it down for them [workshop participants]. That's what they like."

Community service learning with teen dancers as pregnancy prevention teachers in peer trainings was captured in words by Chris, who described the intensity of the experience as follows: "I think it was the first time . . . they were pretty young, and they just really got into it, asking all kinds of questions . . . about C-sections and twins. And it just dawned on many of us—yeah, this is really what this is about."

Notes

1. One-on-one interviews and focus groups were conducted from May to August of 1997 at Moving in the Spirit, Atlanta, Georgia. The names of teen dancers have been changed to protect their identity.

2. For more examples of organizations that accomplish this, see McLaughlin, Irby, and Langman, 1994.

3. For more on mentorship, see Coles, 1993, and Freedman, 1993.

4. For school-based examples of the impact of service on youth development, see Wade, 1997.

5. For more examples, see Lakes, 1997.

6. For more on Freirean themes in community service learning, see Jones, Maloy, and Steen, 1996; Maybach, 1996; and Seigel and Rockwood, 1993.

7. See Freire, 1995, p. 27, for a discussion of related issues.

References

Coles, R. 1993. *The call of service: A witness to idealism.* Boston: Houghton Mifflin.

Freedman, M. 1993. *The kindness of strangers: Adult mentors, urban youth, and the new volantarism.* San Francisco: Jossey Bass.

Freire, P. 1995. *Pedagogy of the oppressed.* New York: Continuum.

Jones, B., R. Maloy, and C. Steen. 1996. Learning through community service is political. *Equity and Excellence in Education,* 29(2): 37–45.

Lakes, R. 1997. *Youth development and critical education: The promise of democratic action.* Albany: State University of New York Press.

Maybach, C. 1996. Investigating urban community needs: Service learning from a social justice perspective. *Education and Urban Society,* 28(2): 224–236.

Maynard, E. 1997. Moving in the Spirit. *VOX: The Voice of Our Generation,* 4(4): 14.

McCord, C. 1995. My daddy is here. *Atlanta Journal-Constitution,* November 5.

McLaughlin, M., M. Irby, and J. Langman. 1994. *Urban sanctuaries: Neighborhood organizations in the lives and futures of inner-city youth.* San Francisco: Jossey Bass.

Pittman, K. 1996. Community, youth, development: Three goals in search of connection. *New Designs for Youth Development,* 12(1): 4–8.

Seigel, S., and V. Rockwood. 1993. Democratic education, student empowerment, and community service: Theory and practice. *Equity and Excellence in Education,* 26(2): 65–70.

Wade, R. (Ed.) 1997. *Community service learning: A guide to including service in the public school curriculum.* Albany: State University of New York Press.

Chapter 8

The Ripples of Empowerment: A Personal Reflection

Joy DesMarais

If your life works, you influence your family.
If your family works, your family influences the community.
If your community works, your community influences the nation.
If your nation works, your nation influences the world.
If your world works, the ripple effect spreads throughout the cosmos.

—Lao-Tse

Understanding the ripples of personal empowerment that occur when young people take on roles as decision makers, implementers, evaluators, leaders, and citizens is important to advancing the service-learning movement. This chapter is a chronicle of the beginning of one such ripple—from being an empowered person to the act of empowering others. In sharing my personal story, I hope that young people will be inspired to take action and adults will be inspired to support such endeavors.

The ripple began as I was preparing for the end of my junior year of high school. The year had been one that challenged my personal expectations concerning education and involvement in leadership activities. I was part of a charter group of students who took part in a school-within-a-school program called Connect-Four at Monticello High School, in Monticello, Minnesota. This program integrated the four disciplines of math, science, social studies, and English in a four-hour block of time, and this led me to question all previous understandings of the disciplines as separate, yet equal. More important, I began to witness four educators become a team of coaches in a game of learning where the playing field expanded from the classroom into the community.

The first year of the program I experienced a new kind of learning, which my teachers referred to as *life-long learning*. They also began to use other words, such as *citizenship, responsibility*, and *self-reliance*. Although I knew the textbook definitions of these words, they began to take on new meaning because of the use of a "new" context—the community.

One of the first experiences with this integration of classroom and real-world learning came as the 1992 elections drew near. An intense, thematic unit designed around this event required us to research and present party platforms and candidates to elementary school students. In an effort to begin building connections with community members, several of us attended the local chapter meeting of the League of Women Voters. This was a planning meeting for the upcoming candidate forum to be held at our high school auditorium. We did not remain observers for long. By the close of the meeting, the candidate forum planning had taken a new shape, and we were becoming integral partners in the process. Before we knew it, we were scheduling candidates, designing questions, coaching student panelists, and arranging for the cable station to record the event for rebroadcast. Every student had a role in which his or her talents were put to use to make the event a success. And a success it was, because citizens young and old came together to participate in the process of American democracy.

At the same time, I experienced leadership in a different dimension. The spring of my sophomore year, I had been elected to a state office in the Minnesota Association of Future Leaders of America/Future Homemakers of America. As this year was coming to an end, I began to feel lost, because I hadn't really thought ahead to what I was going to do once the year was completed. All I had concentrated on for the last three years was becoming a state officer. Once it happened, I enjoyed that opportunity, but I hadn't set any other immediate future goals.

As a state officer, I learned valuable leadership and organizational skills. I also knew those skills needed to be applied and challenged in unique ways for the benefit of my community, enabling others to act and achieve as many other people had inspired me to do. These experiences led me to begin exploring the connections between education and community while weaving an understanding of leadership into the fabric of learning. The opportunity to tie all three—education, community, and leadership—into a work of art came in another creative medium: drama.

In July 1992, I was in Anaheim, California, for the National Conference of FHA/HERO. One of my roles at the conference was to judge student presentations on local community service projects. The one presentation that struck me most was one that opened with a skit performed by two high school students from a violence prevention program in the southern United States. The students presented a skit in which a young woman called her partner to tell him she was pregnant. When the skit ended, its impact on me had just begun. I had a "light-bulb moment." I knew that my school had both an active drama department and a peer-helping program. Tying both together could prove to be a valuable teaching tool for students, by students.

I knew the key to this concept would be student leadership and initiative. Live student drama could be a powerful force for young people to witness just how dangerous drug use could be to their lives. I envisioned students as the actors, directors, and scriptwriters—young people calling the shots to give the program an integrity many other "prevention programs" were missing.

School started in less than two months, and I knew I had some intense brainstorming, goal setting, and visioning to do. I asked myself questions like this: "Does Monticello really need this project?" "Why?" "How could such a project work?" "Would youth be willing to be a part of such a project?" To get diverse perspectives, I asked adults and young people about what they thought of drama as a preventive tool. Some of the adults were skeptical: "Young people are too caught up in their own lives to worry about other people." I disagreed. All of the young people I knew were waiting for a chance to prove that they were capable and responsible, especially for themselves, their peers, and their communities.

As I now reflect on the success of this program, I think finding an adult ally was one of the most important steps I took. I knew this person would have to understand the potential impact a project like this could have on both the student audience and the student leaders involved in its development. To give the project additional credibility, this person also had to have a positive reputation among students.

In Monticello, Tom Keating is known to students and adults as TK. He talks *with* students, not down to them. He is respected among students because he understands the challenges of being young in a complex society. Faculty and staff also have a great deal of trust in him; they allow him to challenge their skeptical conceptions of young people. As the high school's student assistance director, TK is called on to work with every type of student. Helping students in emotional and academic crisis, coaching athletics, and coordinating the peer support and youth service programs are all part of a day in the life of TK.

I had established a solid friendship with TK while working as a peer helper and knew he was someone I could trust to give me honest feedback. The second week of school I went to his office to present my idea. I described to him what I had seen and experienced while in California, and I told him I believed Monticello needed a similar program that was established and run by students, for students. When I finished, his eyes lit up and he had a warm smile on his face. He could hardly sit still. While I had been in Anaheim, TK had been at a drug prevention conference in Minnesota. There he, too, had seen a group of teens perform skits and role plays to encourage their peers to avoid the trap of substance abuse and violence, and he, too, had felt this was an idea with great potential in Monticello. Still more surprising, he had a hunch a student would approach him, ready to take the challenge.

That fall TK and I met weekly to develop our vision of the project. We developed a mission statement and goals. We named our project The Troupe and focused our mission on battling to turn negative choices around, into positive forces for change. We also approached 11 of my classmates to share our idea and invite them to take part. They all accepted.

Our team decided that developing a code of conduct was the first thing we needed to do if we wanted to lay a strong foundation of credibility. It stated that each "Trouper" would not be involved in the use of alcohol, drugs, or tobacco. Being role models, we also agreed not to attend any parties where there was a possibility of such substances being present. This "code" was successful because everyone in the Troupe had a voice in its development; each of us felt accountable. In addition, it was significant for maintaining consistency and integrity, and it set the groundwork for a shared vision—the vision that young people would choose to stay substance and violence free. Team members strove to be positive role models to elementary, middle school, and high school students. We knew that if we were going to have an impact beyond the stage—on the lives of our audience members—we would have to walk the walk, not just talk the talk.

After our last performance of that year, TK and I were approached by students, parents, and teachers to keep the program going into the next year. The feedback was overwhelmingly positive, acknowledging that young people, when given power, can and will make positive changes within their own communities. Five years later, the Troupe has performed for more than 12,000 students and adults across Minnesota, and more than 60 MHS graduates have learned and served as Troupers. In 1995, the Troupe was named one of Minnesota's exemplary service-learning projects by Governor Arne Carlson. Monticello has also made the Troupe a model of youth-led service learning, encouraging other students to develop similar youth-led community and school-based service-learning projects, such as mentoring, tutoring, and other prevention programs.

This experience helped me step into a college career that continues to be filled with service learning and career development. I became fascinated with overall school transformation and was interested in researching examples of school reform similar to that put in place by the Troupe. Toward this end, I approached the Center for School Change at the University of Minnesota's Humphrey Institute of Public Affairs. Through an internship at the Center I was able to make a number of visits to schools with good service-learning programs. Environmental stewardship, mentoring, tutoring, oral history, and student-run entrepreneurial projects were just a few of those I saw in which students were engaged in changing their communities. During many of these site visits, I talked directly with students about their struggles and successes in working with adults. Many said their greatest learning successes and challenges came from having the opportunity to take responsibility for and leadership of all aspects of their projects.

These experiences continued to fuel my interest in school transformation, community development, and youth leadership. My next experience was with the National Youth Leadership Council (NYLC). I began there as a work-study member of the first Youth Project Team— a contemporary approach to youth governance. The purpose was for young people to give the organization input on their points of view, while they gained a greater understanding of the issues facing a national nonprofit organization. It also builds integrity both in and out of NYLC, because in this way the organization is able to incorporate authentic youth voices.

I am now in my senior year in college and in a revised role at NYLC. As the coordinator of Strategic Youth Initiatives, I still work with the Youth Project Team and the capacity building of youth voice within the organization. However, NYLC is taking youth leadership into uncharted waters as it attempts to transform schools and organizations through the F.E.L.L.O.W.S. program, which is funded by the Corporation for National and Community Service. It is our vision that youth-adult partnerships and the initiatives of young people, involving service learning, civic education, and technology, can transform schools as never before. Schools can become institutions for learning, service, leadership, and democracy for all students, by students.

Reflecting on my experience as a young person who has grown from initiating change in my own community to my current role in bringing about school reform and expanding resources for other young people to experience the power of service, I realize there are a number of factors that can serve as lessons to both youth and adults. Thinking about my life lessons and the stories of other young people who have also had transforming service experiences, I am reminded of the impact our ripples can have on one another.

Advice about Developing a Vision for Service

Visions are important insights, guides, and gifts. They help us see what we can truly accomplish. However, every great vision requires a plan. And every great plan must be flexible enough to adapt to the circumstances and environment. As youth are developing a vision for service projects, I recommend having them keep a journal about relevant things they see, hear, feel, and say. These observations will provide important clues about what they should include in their plan. They may hear a great deal of talking from other young people, which could mean they need to listen to the advice of their peers. Or they may be awe-struck by the beauty of nature around them, which could mean they should look into assessing the environmental conditions of their community.

Their plan and vision should include who, what, where, why, when, and how. They must be prepared to do intense research—by having conversations with other people, by assessing their community's needs and assets, and by reading relevant academic information. This may generate questions about details and logistics, but that is fine, because students should also enlist help from adult allies.

Connecting with Adult Allies

Adult allies are important because they provide institutional or organizational power, resources, and knowledge that students are often denied because of age. Adults like TK and the NYLC staff partners work to provide students with such resources. These people also advise and mentor students, which gives young people the opportunity to develop meaningful relationships and work with role models. When looking for allies, youth need to think about adults whose skills, opinions, and attitudes they respect and value. Whom do they trust to be honest with them? Is there a "local expert" concerning the topic they are interested in (e.g., the former newspaper editor for a community history project)? If some similarities and differences complement each other, there will probably be a positive alliance. If, for example, the youth have artistic abilities and interests, and an adult ally has knowledge of the best paints to use in a mural, the relationship will probably be a good one.

Adults often have a difficult time giving up their power. However, when they do, they receive empowerment back tenfold. To know that you played a role in changing the perspective and sense of empowerment of a young person is among the most inspirational feelings one can ever have. This does not mean that if a young person approaches an adult wanting more responsibility and leadership in service endeavors that the adult should just hand over the project. With communication, planning, and strategizing *together*, each person will come to realize the expanded potential in sharing power. Adults must examine and strive to understand the overt and tacit power they hold. Young people, too, must examine the power and idealism they embody in their vision and planning. The power exchange must be transitional, with occasional shifts in the balance until both partners are comfortable in the relationship. It is important to remember that the occasional power imbalance is okay as long as it does not consistently weigh in favor of one of the partners—usually, the adult.

Meaningful Involvement for Young People

In both the Troupe and the Youth Project Team, students govern the program. The team makes every decision by consensus, with some advice from adult mentors. The team is responsible for sustainability issues, such as interviewing and selecting the new team to take their place and examining new needs that arise in the organization and deciding how to meet them. The team also conducts individual and team assessments for training and resource needs. When these needs have been determined, a team will often approach adult mentors for support, advice, and additional resources.

It is critical for service groups to develop a purpose for their ensemble as well as specific goals and expectations. These working documents can be revisited regularly to maintain the group's mission, momentum, and integrity. If group members find that they are not meeting one or more of the desired outcomes, they can revise their plan or establish new guidelines. Adults are not needed to carry out these actions, but they should assist in facilitating the process, asking questions and providing suggestions. It is important to remember that part of learning involves making mistakes!

It is hard to believe that it's been five years since the founding of the Troupe. The experience of planning, implementing, and now leaving the project has changed my life. Initiating a service-learning project has provided me with rich learning experiences and has opened doors of opportunity. Getting those initial experiences in community development and seeing the changes that I helped to create being put into effect instilled me with energy to learn and discover how other young people could also have these experiences. I believe that one of the most powerful lessons in service and leadership is that there is a value in creating opportunities for others to serve, learn, and gain leadership experience. The ripples we create in this way influence the lives around us, and this opens the doors of opportunity and learning for all of us.

Chapter 9

Service Learning and the Making of Small "d" Democrats

Cynthia Parsons

We are faced today with a very curious phenomenon. Our public schools often teach young people about democracy without providing avenues for practice of this important ideal. While our public schools offer academic instruction for every pupil and provide some guidance from schooling to the world of work, they often fall short of their full responsibilities. We are a democracy, and it is the task of our public schools to teach all children not only what that means but how to be democratically active citizens. It is not enough for the schools to provide instruction *about* democracy or to have readings and discussions *about* commerce and industry. Students need to learn to be actively involved in the world about which they are being taught. They must learn to *do* democracy, to use the democratic alphabet, if you will, not just be able to recite it from memory.

Students need to develop the qualities and skills important to carry out meaningful activities in the world around them. They must learn teamwork, problem solving, analysis, orderliness, patience, and other skills and behaviors by employing and exhibiting them in day-to-day situations—not just by talking about them in class. Perhaps even more important than preparing children to make a living is the need for our schools to prepare students for active engagement in a participatory democracy. If all the 18-year-olds in this nation are supposed to know how to carry on the democratic process, they must be given opportunities to practice democracy in school.

It is not enough for schools to hold mock local, state, and national elections, to give paper and pencil tests about democracy in history class, or to form, through the election process, a pseudo student government. This latter habit unfortunately is quite prevalent in U.S. secondary schools. What is formed by elections of class officers is an oligarchy that is anathema to participatory democracy. In only the rarest of instances do student government representatives work out of committee structures and full-school votes on appropriate issues. Sad to say, what students most often learn from in-school elections is that "rule by the few" is the democratic way.

Rule by the few is not an example of the democratic process. What it teaches children is that "someone else" is supposed to solve community problems and that their job as adults is to vote into office whoever they think will do this "best." Our public schools should not just teach children about how to vote but should hold elections and consider referendum questions requiring discussions *and* voting. Administrators, as well as history and social studies teachers, should oversee these activities to make sure that no autocratic methods creep in pretending to be democratic. Someone in every school—why not the top administrators?—should be held accountable for making sure that every child experiences age-appropriate opportunities to participate in democratic decision making.

Democratically literate students are made, not born, and thus our schools need to teach all children how to participate in, preserve, and improve our democracy. Our children need to study community problems and work for their solution in age-appropriate ways in order to become competent, participatory, small "d" democrats. School officials need to take a sincere and fresh look at how they manage school resources and time to provide all students with community service-learning activities that will allow them to integrate academic study with service projects both within and outside of the school setting. The best teaching, whether in or out of the classroom, is interdisciplinary and combines a variety of learning methods and styles. Service learning definitely does this.

What follows is a good example of an age-appropriate lesson in democracy that fits this book's emphasis on critically reflective, activist service learning. A challenge facing most states and school districts in this nation is the need for greater financial equity across districts within state lines. Our democracy calls for a level playing field, including necessary adjustments for those requiring special assistance. Yet few states have gotten it right. In the example that follows, grade school students engage in democratic action in an attempt to solve problems of financial inequality among schools and school districts in the state in which they live. They were given an opportunity to play a role, based on the understanding that creating educational equality in our nation does not come through military orders or authoritarian edicts but rather through a process of democratic decision making engaged in by all citizens.

Practicing Democracy in the Fifth Grade

As part of a school project, fifth graders in a Colorado Springs elementary school studied the town/school budget along with a citizens' group made up of adult volunteers and school administrators. The children discovered that the town was divided into several school districts and that the annual amount of money available to spend per pupil was different in each section of town. This discovery spurred the students to ask the following questions:

- Why is this so? Were those who established the different districts ignorant of the problem? Didn't they know that the children in one district received better schooling than those in the other? Or were they guilty of deliberately fixing district lines so that some children would have better academic and athletic opportunities and equipment than others?
- Was the difference fair? Maybe what looked unfair on paper was fair at the school sites.
- How could the funding be made fair for next year if it wasn't fair this year?

The budget papers showed that the school of the students working on the project had more money than a neighboring school. So a research team of fifth graders made a site visit to one of the schools operating on a smaller budget. There they found an enormous difference in available equipment for coursework, for the arts, and for athletics. They also discovered that no students at that elementary school were studying the school budgets or meeting with adult budget committee members. As one of the team members reflected: "They didn't know about the money; no one let them study the budgets for the different schools."

The fact that young students were part of the study team of a volunteer community budget committee is activist service learning at its very best. The 3 Rs get a good workout by anyone trying to read, compute, and understand a line-item budget. The field study work, which involved researching the coincidence of budget figures with amounts of equipment and quality of operations, was a fantastic way for elementary-level school children to learn measurement skills. Then, back at their home school, they were required to report their findings. What the students learned had to be collated by the team members and correctly summarized. They had to verify findings. They had to show the coincidence of a line-item figure with school features and practices. These fifth graders had to be specific, accurate, and fair.

How many computers did the school with the smaller budget have compared with the number of computers at the larger-budget school? How many overhead projectors? How many bathrooms? How many books in the library? How many television sets with VCR capacity? How much athletic equipment? How many service-learning programs involving peer tutoring? How many service-learning activities taking place out in the community? How many study groups pairing adults with students?

Who decided what to look for? It was the fifth graders themselves and their adult budget committee partners. For several of the fifth graders, the need to know how many pupils were enrolled and then how to determine just how many computers there were per pupil was a very exciting concept. As they explained: "You see, we don't have as many pupils in our building. So, they might have had more computers than we do, but it might not have been as many per pupil. But, sad to say, they didn't have nearly as many computers in their school as we have in ours, they didn't have any special computer teachers like we do, they didn't have a computer lab like we do, and if you divide the number of pupils into the number of computers, wow, it's way smaller!"

As a result of the site visit by the fifth graders and their analysis of budget documents, the students have written letters to newspapers and politicians and publicized their findings. In the process, they have developed important academic skills and have learned about acting on issues of inequality and injustice. Sadly, the adults with a hand in determining differential school budgets in the greater Colorado Springs area have neither changed their autocratic ways nor immediately adopted a more democratic method of school funding. But the issue has not gone away, and the Colorado children have not stopped studying it to learn more about why things are the way they are and how to address the problem.

Research and the Democratic Process

Our youth need to be taught the skills applicable to studying and solving community problems. If, for example, smoking is detrimental to physical well-being, and health problems are more severe for smokers, then young people, as well as adults, need to carry out relevant research projects around the issue of smoking. Our schools have never taken the lead in this matter; they have rarely, for example, been the source of contention that cigarette machines should not be available to any child with the correct change. Some schools have banned smoking in school buildings, but, against all reason, many provide special areas *for* smoking.

Imagine a school that causes students to vote for an autocratic form of governance and at the same time lets students take a democratic vote about smoking! There's never been any question whether smoking is bad for children. Sixty years ago my high school had a demonstration by a state official of what horrible things nicotine from a cigarette did to a linen handkerchief, and we were all required to watch a filmstrip showing the bad effects of cigarette smoking on our lungs. But the smoking issue has not been fully resolved for children or for public schools. I argue that smoking is a community issue, and hence it is a school issue. No student graduates from one of our schools who has not taken a course in general science, and thus it is educators who should provide guidance in how to address the problem while our children are children. The best way to make such teaching effective is through community service-learning activities, integrating academic study with experiential projects. While K–12 students cannot do the types of research conducted by graduate students or scientists in well-financed laboratories, there is much they can do within their community to discover what service-learning activities would best help solve the smoking problem for all school-age young people. They could also address many other critical contemporary issues in the same way.

The following are research concerns crying out for student action in every school district across the nation:

- alcohol consumption and its effects
- equity in school financing and its effects
- use of the democratic process within school governance
- racial and/or cultural integration and its effects
- a curriculum balance placing the arts closer to the center
- fairness in school athletic competitions
- eradication of illiteracy

These are ideal topics for service-oriented research projects that will foster the development of small "d" democrats.

Service and the Democratic Process

Our public schools should be proving grounds for an understanding of participatory as well as representative democracy. And, as has been pointed out since the writing of the Declaration of Independence, our citizens need to know how to read and write to participate fully in our democratic way of life. Thus, literacy is the number one issue facing every public school.

I would like to close this chapter about service learning and the making of small "d" democrats by describing a service-learning program that engages high school students in work with elementary school students to help them learn how to read. Illiteracy is, of course, a nationwide issue. At present our schools fail to teach reading skills to as many as one out of five "typical" children, even though children spend as many as 10 to 12 years in school. This is a scandalous record. It reflects poorly on the school authorities in charge of resources to meet learning needs, it reflects poorly on teachers whose skills prove inadequate, and it certainly causes serious problems in the family, the workplace, and the community. Thus, literacy for all is an important and meaningful goal for young people to address through service.

In a diverse Boston high school, students may take a reading course in which they explore the world of children's literature and are paired with an elementary pupil for the purpose of helping that child learn to read. These pairs, called book buddies, meet regularly as part of a community service-learning project. In the course, the high schoolers learn to evaluate the quality of children's books. They learn which ones empower the imaginations of their book buddies and which do not. They learn the power (or lack of same) of illustrations. They not only study literature in a scholarly way, but they have to write and illustrate their own book, one that will appeal to their "buddy." They also learn about the problems of illiteracy. What does this do for the reading habits of the high schoolers? Let them explain:

"I started reading much better books."

"I began talking with teachers and my parents and their friends about books I should read, and I began reading some of the classics."

"I became really critical about how a story was developed by an author, and when I found a good author, I read more and more of his or her books."

And what about their community service work with the elementary pupils?

"I tried hard to think of a story my buddy would like, and I read lots and lots of books to find the 'perfect' match."

"I knew the book had to be simple to read, but the story had to be interesting or my buddy would be bored. As soon as I found one he really liked, I read through dozens more to find some like that one."

You do not hear many high school students talk about relevance, meaning, and empowerment in reference to their learning—that is, they do not often use those terms. But what these book buddies did achieved much in the way of relevant and empowering service learning. The high schoolers became better readers by studying books written for little kids. And the elementary school kids became better readers because of their book buddies. Both "buddies" were empowered through enhanced literacy.

Research on peer tutoring has taught us that it benefits both those who teach and those who are taught. In the book buddy program, both the little kids and the teenagers improve the range of their vocabularies. Both improve the quality of their reading sophistication. Both enhance their understanding of how to write a description that produces a mental picture. And on and on.

This has direct value for participatory democracy. One cannot be an active participant in a direct democracy without reading ability. And a higher level of literacy—critical thinking—is also important to participate fully in the democratic process. Thus, reading ability and critical-thinking skills combine to produce democratic literacy.

Conclusion

What does all of this have to do with the making of small "d" democrats? These examples illustrate the value of engaging young people in research, reflection, and service as elements of practicing democracy. The fifth graders studying school budgets in Colorado Springs had to consider questions of equity and justice as they carried out their research and analysis. The high school book buddies had to be reflective and caring in analyzing books and understanding the needs of their young reading partners to be successful with them. In both cases, the young people had to question, investigate, and act on their world to accomplish their service goals. In the process, the literacy of participatory democracy was engaged and developed.

Chapter 10

Building Legacies: School Improvement and Youth Activism in an Urban Teacher Education Partnership

Robert W. Maloy, Abbie Sheehan, Irene S. LaRoche, and Richard J. Clark, Jr.

leg.a.cy \ *n. pl* -cies
Something received from an ancestor or predecessor
or from the past.

At 2:30 on a cold mid-January afternoon, six ninth graders and two teachers gather together on the stage of their school's main auditorium. They are members of the Central Academy Theatrical Company, a newly formed after-school drama group that is readying a production of Shakespeare's A Midsummer Night's Dream *for a March performance. The students are excited; today's rehearsal is a walk-through of a key scene just before the end of Act 1.*

As they complete their voice and body warm-ups, the group wonders aloud about the whereabouts of one of the cast members, the young woman playing the part of Hermia, who, unbeknownst to them, has been delayed by having to pick up an assignment from a teacher after class. Suddenly she appears in the doorway at the far end of the hall. As she makes her way toward the stage, the students see her and break into spontaneous cheers and applause, which she returns with equal enthusiasm. It is a powerful moment; rarely in schools today do students applaud and cheer one other as they arrive for a learning activity.

A Midsummer Night's Dream is the only student theater production of the year at Central Academy, a school poised, like the one thousand ninth graders who attend it, midway between middle school and high school. There are few extracurricular or after-school activities here, but the drama group has been meeting twice a week since October, and it will increase that time to five days a week of rehearsals as the performance time draws near. They have virtually no budget for the production; the student actors dress in their everyday clothes and perform on a stage with only a bench and a wooden log for props. Still, they exhibit great affection for the play's rich language and symbolism, because, as one of the cast members notes, "Midsummer takes place in the halls of our school every day."

These ninth grade performers were directed by two graduate students who were spending the year teaching at the academy's main building, Central High School, as part of 180 Days in Springfield, a combined master's degree and secondary teacher education program conducted by the University of Massachusetts, Amherst, and the Springfield (Massachusetts) Public Schools. While the theater group was doing Shakespeare, 10 other after-school or cocurricular projects were under way at the high school and at one middle school under the guidance of 12 other 180 Days graduate students plus four university undergraduates who wanted to work with youth in schools.

Projects included a writing and acting club, a young women's support group, a living history activity, a community violence prevention effort, a math/science/technology career day, a computer club, a gymnastics/dance group, a girls' basketball clinic, and a girls' cheerleading squad. These leadership efforts became known as *legacy projects* after the principal at the Chestnut Accelerated Middle School for the Visual and Performing Arts challenged the college students to create learning activities that would meet real needs of young people while making a lasting impact on schools.

In this chapter, we describe the results of this year-long legacy project experiment in our urban school–university teacher education partnership. For the first time at our campus, a teacher education program invited secondary-teacher-certification candidates and undergraduate students interested in school change to organize and conduct school improvement, community service learning (CSL), or youth leadership/ activism projects as a formal part of their academic program of study. The impact of legacy projects on those prospective teachers, on the middle and high school students who participated in the activities, and on ourselves as teacher educators is the story we seek to tell. It is an account of profound and unexpected learning for all of us, with many implications for how to empower youth and prepare new teachers in schools today.

Changing the "Job Descriptions" of Teachers and Students

Asking teacher certification candidates to design and develop a legacy project was a conscious effort on the part of the designers of 180 Days in Springfield to change the "job description" of the beginning teacher. As extensive ethnographic literature on teacher education has demonstrated, students preparing to teach often feel caught "between tradition and change" (Britzman, 1991, 29–30). While college-level teacher preparation courses typically introduce promising best practices, such as project-based learning, student decision making about curriculum topics, and authentic assessments based on portfolios, new teachers still spend considerable amounts of time acquiring teaching "skills," largely through "imitation, recitation, and assimilation." In so doing, they form "an image of knowledge as 'received' and an identity of the neophyte as an empty receptacle."

A tendency toward traditional methodologies is reinforced during student teaching as new teachers struggle to master a repertoire of classroom strategies while trying to become effective within existing regularities and personalities of a school's culture. Innovative best practices wash out amidst the pressures of trying to pull together curriculum materials, instructional methods, and classroom management strategies. Simply trying to survive, many novices focus on "control," avoiding controversial discussions or new approaches while emphasizing fragmented facts, dull worksheets, and multiple-choice tests (McNeil, 1986).

We wondered how conducting school improvement, community service-learning (CSL), or youth leadership projects with young people might affect the ways new teachers think about themselves as secondary school educators. Such projects necessarily place certification candidates (and college students interested in tutoring and mentoring in schools) in new relationships with students outside of the structured classroom environment. They must serve as coaches or facilitators of student learning rather than instructors of academic content.

Our plan surfaced key questions: Do new teachers gain new insights about learning and teaching by organizing legacy projects as part of their teacher preparation program? Are their attitudes and behaviors as educators influenced by involvement with youth in nonclassroom, less formally structured learning settings? Do they plan to incorporate new approaches or changes into their teaching as a result of their roles as legacy project developers and leaders? Do new teachers see young people in new ways or regard them as having different talents and capabilities after participating with them in project activities?

Changing the roles of middle and high school youth from passive students to active learners was another, though perhaps less explicitly stated, part of the design of 180 Days in Springfield. Educational observers from John Goodlad's classic study (1984) to more recent critiques (Johnson, 1990, and Shor, 1996) have found a remarkable sameness to the 7,000 hours that adolescents spend in middle and high schools. Classroom routines proceed with few opportunities for students to find connections between academic subjects and issues in their lives and communities. One report asked readers to imagine themselves as a secondary school student:

> Every 50 minutes, perhaps 6 or 7 times each day, assemble with 30 or so of your peers, each time in a different group, sit silently in a chair in neat, frozen rows, and try to catch hold of knowledge as it whizzes by you in the words of an adult you met only at the beginning of the school year. The subject of one class has nothing to do with the subject of the next class. If a concept is confusing, don't ask for help, there isn't time to explain. If something interests you deeply, don't stop to think about it, there's too much to cover. (Carnegie Council on Adolescent Development, 1989, 37)

As with the college students preparing to become teachers, we had key questions about the potential impacts of legacy projects on secondary school youth. How would students make sense of their participation and involvement in learning activities that were new to them and to their schools? Would they interact differently with other students and the outside-of-school community? Would opportunities emerge for them to learn positive ways to analyze information, to make personal judgments, and to link past experiences to current issues in their lives?

We also wondered about the possibilities for "youth activism" within the projects. Conceptually, getting young people actively engaged in after-school activities opens up opportunities for them to become agents of change in their school and community. Looking at service-learning programs, Richard Lakes (1996, 134) has proposed that the roles of youth in educational activities can be shifted dramatically when "the pedagogical project becomes a vehicle for transformative learning." Then, students participate in activities that "challenge comfortable taken-for-granted understandings about self and society." How might this happen, even tentatively, in the legacy projects at Central High School, Central Academy, and Chestnut Middle School?

Developing Legacy Projects

The 1996–97 academic curriculum for 180 Days in Springfield included a year-long course entitled "Curriculum, Methods and Programs in Urban Education." As part of this course, each teacher certification candidate was asked to plan and implement a school improvement, community service learning, or youth leadership project with middle and high school students. Projects could take place during or after school; all would represent significant value added to the schools in terms of initiatives that would most likely not be happening without the energy and leadership of the candidates. Requiring novice teachers to initiate improvement and service projects was a new idea, not previously part of any University of Massachusetts, Amherst, teacher education program.

The course began by introducing the 180 Days candidates to the state-mandated School Improvement Plans (SIPs) developed at Chestnut Middle School and Central High School, settings where all candidates were spending their year of teacher preparation. As part of the Massachusetts Educational Reform Act of 1993, all schools in the state must implement continuous school improvement plans. As a visual and performing arts magnet school, Chestnut's SIP priorities included infusing the arts into all curriculum areas as well as further integration of school change initiatives in the areas of peer mediation, talented and gifted education, and the advisor-advisee program. Priorities at Central also included the arts as well as career awareness, academic enhancement, and parent/community involvement.

Following the SIP overviews, students and course instructors, one a university faculty member and the other a school principal, agreed that each school improvement, CSL, youth leadership project would address academic enrichment and service learning priorities established by teachers and administrators in their building's school improvement plans; involve a group of middle or high school students who voluntarily choose to participate, either during or after school; and include—whenever possible—performances, products, or presentations by secondary students to wider audiences of students, teachers, parents, and other community members.

All school improvement activities had to be approved by the school principal as well as the university instructor of the course. The principals added that each project must be shared with Chestnut or Central's School-Centered Decision-Making Team so that teachers and parents would be aware of these new activities.

The following 11 legacy projects were conducted by 180 Days candidates and undergraduate students from the university. They involved more than 200 middle and high school students as regular participants. Most met on Wednesdays and Thursdays (and sometimes Mondays) from 2:15 to 3:15, when the late bus arrived.

Computer/Technology Club (Chestnut Middle School, organized by two 180 Days candidates)

Middle school students used Chestnut's newly created computer laboratory after school on Mondays, Wednesdays, and Thursdays. The popularity of computer club soon created a need for before-school sessions as well. More than 40 students regularly used the machines for personal and academic projects, and teachers appreciated students' increased abilities to navigate computers and their improved understanding of the roles of technology in schools and society.

Central Academy Theatrical Company (Central Academy, organized by two 180 Days candidates)

The after-school Central Academy Theatrical Company involved 20 ninth graders rehearsing and performing Shakespeare's *A Midsummer Night's Dream*. A video of their public performance was donated to Central High School as a teaching resource.

Writing and Acting Club (Chestnut Middle School, organized by two university undergraduates)

The Writing and Acting Club offered 20 sixth and seventh graders opportunities to write and perform their own compositions on Wednesday and Thursday afternoons. As the 1997 spring semester progressed, some Monday afternoon meetings were added at the students' request. The group also produced a publication of their poetry, stories, and essays and made it available to all the middle schools in Springfield.

Investigating Math, Science, and Technology in Our Community Day (Central High School, organized by three 180 Days candidates)

A group of 20 high school students and three teachers spent more than two months planning and organizing a career day in which two dozen speakers from local businesses, industry, and colleges came to the high school for a morning of presentations and discussions about mathematics and science in careers and personal development. More than a thousand high school students attended.

Girls' Basketball Clinic (Chestnut Middle School, organized by one 180 Days candidate)

A clinic was formed for 12 girls who were just beginning to play basketball and wanted to learn the fundamentals of the game. Practices and intramural games were held Monday, Wednesday, and Thursday afternoons from January to June. The group met a glaring need at Chestnut; prior to this, the school had no organized basketball program for girls.

Chestnut Eagle Cheerleaders and Homework Club (Chestnut Middle School, organized by one 180 Days candidate)

This 12-member girls' cheerleading squad met after school on Mondays, Wednesdays, and Thursdays. Initially, the focus was just cheerleading. But as the year progressed and students expressed difficulty in keeping up with the demands of their school work, a decision was made to spend some of the after-school time doing homework together. The rest of the time was devoted to practicing for the squad's performances at the boys' basketball games.

Sisters (Chestnut Middle School, organized by two university undergraduates)

The group calling themselves Sisters met every Wednesday afternoon beginning in September and continuing throughout the school year. The goal for these 11 seventh and eighth graders was to explore issues of personal identity and self-concept. In addition to discussing adult-chosen topics, the girls talked about whatever was on their minds. Sisters produced collage posters and a videotape on topics discussed in the group and shared these materials with the school.

Gymnastics Club (Chestnut Middle School, organized by two 180 Days candidates)

Gymnastics started slowly because of the need to clarify school rules about the use of equipment, but once begun, the facilitators had to create two separate groups to meet the large turnout of 35 boys and girls. The club met on Monday, Wednesday, and Thursday afternoons from March to June. Group activities were connected to the school's health and science curriculums, and students led stretching and warm-up exercises.

Living History Project (Central High School, organized by one 180 Days candidate)

The Living History Project was an interdisciplinary, in-school, after-school project worked on by one tenth-grade English class. They invited seven Vietnam-era veterans to share experiences of the war. Each student interviewed one of the veterans. The interviews were transformed into biographies, stories, and poems for a student publication called *Images from the Past: Stories from Vietnam*. Copies were given to other English and history classes as well as to the school library as a curriculum resource.

Bilingual Tutoring and Mentoring (Chestnut Middle School, organized by one 180 Days candidate)

Bilingual Tutoring and Mentoring was originally intended to be a tutoring center for Latino students. Because of transportation problems, however, University of Massachusetts bilingual tutors were unable to join the group. A half-dozen Latino students did receive in-school and after-school assistance from the group organizer, who was also a first-language Spanish speaker.

413 Promotion and Marketing Street Team (Central High School, organized by one 180 Days candidate)

The Street Team met after school and on Saturdays throughout the school year to promote special events for Springfield's African-American community. A primary concern of the 10-member group was the issue of violence in the community and in the rap and hip-hop music enjoyed by many adolescents. Students examined the messages in song lyrics, invited people from the music industry to discuss marketing and careers, and organized events for youth.

New Roles, New Settings, New Insights

To research legacy projects carried out under the auspices of 180 Days in Springfield, we looked at their influence on the professional education of new teachers and their impact on the school experience of middle and high school students. Certification candidates and university undergraduates documented their projects by keeping a portfolio of information about design and delivery of activities. A middle school teacher from Chestnut (one of the coauthors of this chapter) was an ongoing researcher and project documentor. She visited every project at least twice to observe firsthand what was happening. She also interviewed middle and high school student participants and college student legacy organizers to find out how the projects were affecting them as students and teachers.

Voices of New Teachers

In retrospect, 180 Days candidates were of two minds about their participation in legacy projects. Several cited projects as one hallmark of the program and urged that they be continued as a requirement for certification. For some, the project was their most compelling learning experience as a new teacher. All agreed that it had been hard to "fit it all in" their busy schedules. They spoke about the difficulties of juggling multiple responsibilities—teaching classes, meeting with students, planning with cooperating teachers, taking graduate courses—and then organizing their project on top of these commitments.

Even the rigors of undergraduate college had not prepared most candidates for the high-pressure world of teaching in a secondary school. They recalled feeling frustrated at different points in the year about the teacher certification program, which placed complex and competing demands on them in their first months in education. Also, they were displeased by the intricacies of school system and university bureaucracies: planning a field trip or being reimbursed for expenses proved to be daunting tasks as the candidates had to deal with permission slips, scheduling conflicts, and rules about what funding sources or grant monies would pay for a bus or buy supplies for club members.

New approaches to teaching were on the minds of some 180 Days candidates reflecting on their legacy projects. For two, leadership experiences in their after-school Shakespeare project directly affected how they conducted their classes. One science teacher decided to structure her in-school classes more like the after-school theater club, giving students greater freedom, choice, and input while still maintaining clear rules and accountabilities. "I have learned to ease up a little, to be more flexible," she observed. Her after-school partner, an English teacher, found that the same preparation and organization he used after school benefited his in-school classes. He successfully implemented there some of the same discussion topics and acting techniques he used with the theater group. The after-school drama project created new ways for him to teach literature.

For another 180 Days candidate, legacy projects became an opportunity to experiment with teaching outside the established curriculum. Dissatisfied with the way her school's world history textbook portrayed African Americans, a black social studies teacher sought "to give my students control" of their learning. Her 413 Promotion and Marketing Street Team project focused on high school youth making a difference in the community through positive change. "Participating in a legacy project makes you realize that school doesn't end at 2:30," she said. "What we do and learn beyond the classroom is just as important as what we are exposed to in school."

Several members of 180 Days in Springfield felt the legacy projects served to legitimize their position as a teacher in the school. As first-year educators who were also in a university certification program, the candidates wondered whether they were viewed by their students and veteran faculty as "real" teachers or just college interns. Legacy projects provided them with formal activities to organize and implement as new teachers, reducing role confusion for some of them. One math teacher candidate remarked, "Kids would say 'I have basketball with Mr. D,' and this would provide an air of credibility to my place in the building."

Candidates repeatedly cited the significance of being in charge of their legacy project. During student teaching in the first part of the year and to some extent during second semester clinical teaching, candidates had to implement the curriculum of their cooperating teacher. They used lesson plans and instructional materials designed by others. By contrast, from the outset legacy projects consisted mainly of their own ideas. The feelings of confidence derived from these experiences carried over to their classroom teaching. "After all," noted one candidate, "I am alone with 20 kids after school and things are working fine, so I can handle kids in school as well."

Almost everyone in 180 Days expressed surprise at the behaviors and attitudes of students during the legacy projects. "There is a different atmosphere after school," said one candidate. Adolescents often acted and responded in more self-responsible and thoughtful ways. Some seemed to be happily engaged in "academic" activities for the first time. Even the candidates themselves admitted that they behaved one way in their projects and another way in their classes. They, too, were having fun, interacting productively with students. They looked forward to after-school time.

Their own good feelings, and the behaviors of students during projects, raised puzzling questions among the new teachers. "How can I tap into this side of my student during school?" wondered one candidate. They had no ready-made answers to the question. The concepts of service learning, youth leadership, and student decision making sound fine theoretically as ways to promote new responses by adolescents, but these new teachers indicated they had few strategies for implementing these ideas within the norms and structures of regular classrooms. Most backed away from openly questioning the formal structure of schools while continuing to wonder about how to go beyond conventional approaches.

Voices of Students

For middle and high school students, the legacy projects were a new feature of their school experience. Most came to clubs and projects warily, not sure this was going to be a good thing. Once involved, though, they repeatedly said they did not want the activities to end. Overwhelmingly, adolescents from Chestnut, Central Academy, and Central said they valued the projects because "they gave me something to do after school." For many middle schoolers, in particular, going to basketball practice, computer club, or gymnastics gave them a place to be away from the streets.

The school performance of students received a boost from their project participation. The schools required students to be in class all day in order to attend an after-school activity. Most project organizers also insisted that students maintain passing grades. Many youngsters freely admitted that they came to school to go to their after-school club. For some it was fun; for others it was the satisfaction of doing something they liked to do. One middle schooler explained, "My grandma has a whole wall in the living room where she hangs everything that me and [my sister] do in school. Everything I do in writing club she hangs. I try to bring her home something every week." Teachers noted that some students' overall academics improved because of the importance they placed on being part of a club or project. "What did you do with José?" one teacher asked the writing club facilitators after José's classwork got dramatically better.

Many students cited "choice" and "confidence" as reasons why they enjoyed being part of a legacy project. The idea that "I am in charge, and I am making the decision to attend" differs dramatically from normal classroom situations, in which they have few opportunities to exercise choice as part of their school day. Others admitted that they acted differently in these projects. "It helps me focus," said one student; "it makes you learn responsibility," reported another. Some suggested their more controlled behaviors after school translated back into more responsible behavior during school. Others indicated they felt better about themselves: "After reciting Shakespeare," said one youngster, "I can do anything."

Some students acknowledged seeing teachers in a new way—not so much as the enemy but as separate individuals who were interested in some of the same things that students were interested in. For more than a few students, the contrast between experiences in legacy projects and experiences in classrooms and corridors came down to a simple, yet profound, delineation: "The teachers are nice, they don't yell at you." Others found satisfaction in how they were listened to by legacy project organizers. As one student remarked: "Well, see, you are letting us say mean things about the club, well, not mean, but, you know, what we don't like, and you're not getting mad and asking us to leave."

From Student Involvement to Youth Activism

Every legacy project became a focal point of the school day for its student participants. On visiting a project, the energy, enthusiasm, and commitment of students was readily apparent. Everyone was talking, laughing, thinking, and learning together in vibrant communities of discourse. And real school improvement goals were being addressed. Previously, the middle school hardly provided athletics for girls, no one at the high school had the time to organize a math/science career day or ninth grade drama, and so on.

The active involvement of students in projects created leadership opportunities. As they encountered adults in new, unfamiliar relationships outside the formal authority of established classrooms, teacher roles, and school-day schedules, students developed new responses. Together with the college students who were their teachers, youth began to exercise leadership by taking responsibility for project goals, solving problems collaboratively, assessing their own activities, and applying what they learned to their own lives as members of a school

and a community. In most projects, students believed they were partners with adults in the design and delivery of group activities—in sharp
contrast with the way they saw many of their regular school classes.

In at least four of the projects—Writing and Acting Club, Sisters,
413 Street Team, and the ninth grade theatrical company—student
leadership became youth activism. Through these projects, students
explored self-chosen issues of social justice and personal identity formation, exercised their voice in group decision making, expressed their
ideas to external audiences through publications and performances,
and worked for change in school and neighborhood communities.
Although the themes of justice, identity, decision making, audience,
and change were present in all of the legacy projects to some extent,
students in these four projects combined these features of youth activism in especially creative ways.

The Writing and Acting Club

The Chestnut Writing and Acting Club met after school on Wednesday and Thursday afternoons throughout the second half of the year.
The club was organized by two undergraduate students, Celina and
Andalib. Both were social thought and political economy majors at
the university. Celina had spent the previous semester at Chestnut
tutoring culturally and linguistically diverse students through the
University's TEAMS Project. She decided to do an after-school project
for her senior honors thesis and then enlisted Andalib to work with
her.

The Writing and Acting Club began tentatively; only one seventh
grader came to the first scheduled meeting. She wrote eight poems
that afternoon and told her friends about the group. Celina and Andalib
then posted signs announcing the club and began recruiting students
in the sixth and seventh grade classes where Celina was tutoring during the school day. Soon a consistent group of 20 youth began attending—8 girls and 12 boys, 11 of whom were African American, 8 Latino
and 1 white.

From the outset, Celina and Andalib wanted to create an after-
school space where students could openly express their ideas and feelings. But asking 20 young adolescents to sit down and begin writing
about their experiences growing up and going to school in Springfield
was not an option. Virtually all of the youngsters who came said they
did not like to write—at least in the ways they were asked to do so in
school. The two college students also wanted to explore issues of

social justice and personal identity formation with urban youth. But seldom had these youngsters shared writing about themselves or their lives with teachers or tutors.

Celina and Andalib started the club with a combination of music, food, thoughtful discussions, and individual choices for self-expression. Their idea was to blend these elements to create group experiences. One day, for example, it was proposed to club members that before anyone had anything to eat, each person would say one thing they were proud of about themselves. Writing topics were similarly suggested and agreed to by everyone.

Decision making became a collective process, with students exercising their voice in the operation of the club. A vivid example of this was the noise and commotion that obstructed anyone trying to get the attention of the whole group. Free from the orderly rows and single-file lines of in-school routines, the students were happy expressing themselves loudly and physically. Reading aloud was especially difficult; at times everyone seemed to be talking at once as a writer tried to share what she or he had written.

While acknowledging the noise problem, the students stated they did not want Celina or Andalib to impose control by speaking loudly to the group. They also objected strongly to raising hands for permission to speak. Hand raising and loud voices, constant features of their school days, carried with them intense feelings of institutional and adult control. After some puzzling about what to do, the group agreed that individuals would raise a fist high into the air to signal everyone to silence. Collectively-raised fists were seen as different from individual hands as a way to communicate to the group.

The first writing involved acrostic poems about friends and families. The simplicity of the form and the hidden words inside the lines made it an appealing form of poetic communication. Confidence with and enjoyment of writing led to poems about personal experiences in urban communities, such as this African-American youngster's acrostic using the word "justice":

Just stand up for yourself and make sure that people like
Us have justice
Stand
Tall and be
Independent
Cause you will succeed and
Enrich in justice.

As the club progressed, students expanded their explorations of social issues in short personal thought essays, including one entitled "Racism, in My Eyes," which included these lines:

> I feel equal when kids of different colors don't look down on me like I'm nothing. Little kids (about 6 and down) don't understand racism. They don't show color hatred because they don't know it. Little kids learn racism from their parents, friends, role models, or just the people around them. The things they hear and see, they show.

Another young writer wondered: "souls are lost because of violence, kids get injured because of gangs, why use violence to solve problems?"

In April, the Writing and Acting Club spent a day at the university. The youngsters took a tour of the campus, talked with staff from the Admissions Office, ate lunch at the Campus Center, and read their poetry and stories to a group of college students in one of the dormitories. Shortly after the trip, the club members decided to assemble their writings in a book. Collectively, they wrote and edited *Words of Wisdom: Chestnut Poems, Stories, and Essays, 1997*. When the 42-page anthology was completed, they sent a copy to all the middle school libraries in Springfield. The dedication page said:

> The Writing members think the best things about the writing club are that we get to express ourselves and speak our minds about things. The Writing Club teaches us to be more independent, responsible and how to write better and how to solve problems without using violence. This is our book that we worked hard on and we hope you enjoy it.

413 Marketing and Promotion Street Team

When Shannan heard that her 180 Days in Springfield program would include the development of after-school projects with students, she knew exactly what she would do. She decided to use her legacy project to create the 413 Marketing and Promotion Street Team. The Street Team combined student interest in music with the development of marketing and advertising skills for the music and recording industries. Shannan's goal was to teach real-world business procedures while promoting positive self-images among young African Americans.

In October, Shannan approached students she thought would be interested in her idea. The initial group of three or four quickly grew to 16. Shannan attributed this to the recruitment efforts of the students; their first job was to promote the Street Team itself. She also noted that "the students in my classes observed me interacting in a more personal way with students from the Street Team and they wanted to be a part of it. They just wanted some special treatment. Like after class, I might say to Shepella, 'Can I talk to you?' and I think they wanted to be in the know." Shannan took the definition of youth involvement beyond the other legacy projects; she had students on the Street Team from four different high schools in the area.

In contrast with traditional school structures, where many students regard the teacher as an authority figure who limits their creativity and self-expression, Shannan felt strongly that the students in the Street Team should determine their own goals and directions. "I really didn't want to tell them how to do things but more or less guide them," she explained. "It's kind of fun because they don't need my permission to do anything." She provided support and advice, but left decision making to them. At times, Shannan did not agree with their decisions, such as that to put a cap on membership. Shannan felt that the Street Team should be open to all students, but the group explained to her that with smaller numbers they could work closely with each other and ensure accountability of all members. Shannan contributed her advice, but ultimately the students made the choice to limit the size of the group.

The majority of the group's projects were centered around music, and they also provided the advertising for the ninth grade school play. But as the year progressed, the students decided to include community change issues as part of the Street Team's action agenda. This led them to consider the problem of violence in their communities. With the recent violent deaths of two hip-hop musicians, the connection to their original focus was clear. The students went beyond the promoting and marketing of music-oriented school/community events to organizing their own activities that focused on building a more peaceful community.

They decided to hold a panel discussion on violent themes in hip-hop and rap music. Shannan used her connections to the music industry to help secure professional speakers. The students did all of the work in organizing the event, including seeking local business sponsors, handling publicity, and determining the format for the day. The students felt that their efforts toward peace should involve the entire community, so they decided to hold the panel discussion at a neighboring business rather than at the school. Promotion of the panel was also done on a communitywide level.

One outgrowth of the panel discussion was the idea that youth need somewhere to go after school that offers both safety and enriching activities. The Street Team decided to work toward creating these places for Springfield youth. They organized dances and music events with the theme of keeping the peace and getting youth off the streets. These events were a huge success, with attendance well into the hundreds at the team's end-of-the-school-year dance.

When asked why the Street Team was important to them, one student responded, "We all like hip-hop and R&B, so it's fun, and we get to plan a lot of the stuff. It's like we're in charge." Another youth said, "We feel like we count. No one is comin' down on us, it's like we get back whatever we put in." A third liked the opportunity to review new music, noting that "very important people at recording studios care about what we think." Shannan has graduated from 180 Days, but her students in the Street Team have decided to continue their work and have remained active throughout the summer and fall.

Sisters
Sisters was developed by Kim and Ligaya, two undergraduate nursing students from the university, and Martha, a second-year English teacher at Chestnut Middle School, to educate seventh and eighth grade girls about personal health issues. Ligaya was a tutor at the school through the university's TEAMS Project, and she used her contacts with students to recruit young women to Sisters. A group of 12 girls met with Kim, Ligaya, and Martha on Wednesday afternoons throughout the school year.

Based on their nursing courses, research on urban youth, and conversations with students, Kim and Ligaya decided to concentrate on body image and its impact on self-concept. While adults chose this general focus, weekly discussion topics were decided by the students. These arose from the issues and concerns they were facing, including sexually transmitted diseases, family/relationship abuse, sexual harassment, and eating disorders. Sisters became a safe place for the young women to discuss their experiences in and outside of school. It offered emotional support that many of the students were lacking elsewhere in their lives. As one youngster explained, "[the group] teaches us to respect ourselves as women and teaches us to show people how to respect us as women."

Kim, Ligaya, and Martha started by exploring issues of personal identity formation. Each student created an identity collage about herself on posterboard and shared it with the group. This multiracial collaboration included four Latina and eight African-American students along with one Asian and two white teachers. Together, they tied many issues into their collages. Eating disorders and body issues came to the surface as topics that needed attention. Many of the young women were concerned about their appearance. Negative self-image was a common theme; one student even confessed to occasionally depriving herself of food.

Kim and Ligaya added their knowledge of nutrition and health to the discussion. From their own research, the students developed materials to share with other young women in the community to educate them about eating disorders. The group constructed a larger-than-life food guide pyramid to use as a teaching visual aid. They created a videotape that included presentations by individual students as well as a large group discussion on the topic of youth and healthy eating choices. The students hoped that sharing their knowledge and materials would help educate other young women in the school community.

As the year progressed, Kim and Ligaya saw important changes in the young women in the group. One youngster "would only speak to her cousin, who also came each Wednesday, for the first month. Now she walks into the room as if it were her own." At different times members of the group would step into leadership roles, speaking assertively on the topic under discussion or helping the other girls to respond respectfully to one another. From week to week the girls shifted the focus of their conversations whenever a member needed to talk about a problem, as when one young woman was fearful of going home to a potentially explosive family situation. The other girls gave her advice from their own experiences and offered their support. Subsequently, Martha gave everyone a confidential address book in which the students wrote each other's nicknames and phone numbers for use outside the group time.

When asked about Sisters, the students said they valued the opportunity to share feelings and confidences with other young girls and adult women. One girl said of the group, "[It] gives you a time where you can have fun and be yourself; it helps you learn about women's issues; it gives you a chance to talk about your problems and solve them." Another group member commented that "[Sisters] gives kids a good thing to do instead of being out getting into trouble." A third youngster, noting a contrast with her regular classes, said, "We learned more about what life is all about." A fourth said the most important thing she learned during the year was "how to be independent."

Central Academy Theatrical Company

Until September 1997, when the two buildings merged, Central Academy was the ninth grade component of Springfield Central High School. It was located about a mile and half away from the main school building. The academy was considered part of the high school, but given the distance, many of the extracurricular activities that were part of the regular high school were not available to the ninth graders. One of the missing extracurriculars was a student drama club. Two 180 Days interns, Heather (a science teacher) and Mike (an English teacher), decided to fill this gap for the ninth graders.

Heather and Mike started by organizing an after-school drama workshop for about 20 students in late September 1996. They began the group with modest goals: "to know movement, reading, learn a bit of Shakespeare, and work on their imagination." At the end of eight weeks, said Heather, "we had a Shakespeare Day where we had copied small scenes, and we had the kids read them." The youth chose the scenes they wanted to read, and virtually all of them decided that they wanted to be part of a student performance of *A Midsummer Night's Dream*.

Rehearsals ran from January to mid-March and were held two days a week to start, soon expanding to five days a week and some weekends. As Heather, Mike, and the young performers talked about the script, the students began to make connections between the storyline and aspects of their life at school. They recognized that gossip, intrigue, and romantic entanglements in the play have many parallels with the daily life of high school students. One student noted: "It's things we deal with every day—this boy liking that girl; that girl liking a different boy. It's funny."

Heather and Mike decided not to run the play strictly by the script but to turn it over to the students so they could include individual perspectives. They called a cast meeting and said they wanted to do a modern version of the show but were worried about Shakespeare's use of magic to explain how various things happen. Mike said, "'There's no magic in modern days, is there?' And so we let them decide what they thought was the explanation, and they said it was a dream." The students decided to situate the opening of their play in a summer school classroom, where contemporary ninth graders drifted into a fantastic reverie and assumed the roles of Shakespeare's characters. Then the students began lively discussions about their roles and the motivation of their characters.

Peer feedback and support were an essential component of rehearsals. Heather and Mike originally held review sessions at the end of
each day, but modified this approach as the students took ownership
of providing positive reinforcement and critique throughout rehearsal.
When one student, frustrated in her attempts to recall a line, exclaimed,
"I can't do anything off-book yet!" another student quickly responded,
"You're doing great!" A sense of accountability was built through this
group process, and students recognized that a missed rehearsal meant
not only that the absent individual lost out but that the whole cast
suffered as well.

Collective decision making and a heightened awareness of who was
their audience for the play characterized rehearsals. In performing a
modern production with a dream sequence, the students had decided
to take an active role in changing the atmosphere at the school, using
the play as a medium through which to express their ideas. They saw
themselves commenting on how students interact with one another as
well as critiquing school practices in general.

For the students, the drama group created many different learning
experiences. "This is the first time I can honestly say I understand
Shakespeare," one actor said laughingly, before adding, "No, I mean I
get it; I really get it." Another student said, "Before I joined drama, I
didn't know any of the breathing exercises and enunciation." A third
noted, "At first, it's confusing with all the thees and thous. The language is weird. It's hard to talk that way because you don't feel right
doing it. But once you get the story and you know what's going on, it's
a lot easier."

The final production of the play was performed for two enthusiastic audiences, during the day for students and again in the evening for
students, parents, and other members of the community. For the students, having the whole school as an audience was a personally satisfying experience. One performer said, "It also gives you confidence.
You have to be confident that your lines are memorized, and some of
us have mad amounts of lines to memorize. Also you can't be afraid to
speak in public." Another student remarked, "It's something for us as
a school to take pride in."

Leadership, Activism, and Change

Looking back over a year of legacy projects in our 180 Days in Springfield partnership, what have we learned about new teacher prepara-

tion, youth activism, and school change? We offer the following thoughts for those who are engaged in teacher education, service learning, and youth leadership development.

First, the projects provided a powerful experience for prospective teachers—both graduate students preparing to teach through 180 Days and undergraduates tutoring and mentoring young people in school. They gained new insights into adolescent behaviors and discovered fresh approaches to classroom organization and teaching methods. They found themselves in roles that required new negotiating skills with schools as organizations and bureaucracies. More subtle but perhaps most important, they reported added confidence, respect from experienced colleagues, and a sense of efficacy as a result of their legacy work. Furthermore, they saw significant differences in their own and their students' attitudes and behaviors in the less formal project contexts as compared with formal classroom settings.

Second, legacy projects tapped a tremendous reservoir of commitment among middle and high school youth. Students wanted to be part of efforts that made sense to them. These high schoolers and middle schoolers were looking for opportunities to express their ideas and values, make genuine decisions, and institute changes in the world around them. As educators, we need to continually search for ways to get youth engaged in personally meaningful activities where they can be directors of their own learning and activists in the improvement of their schools and communities.

Third, through words and actions, some middle and high school youth began using their legacy projects as vehicles for social change. Writing club members wrote frankly about racism, justice, and their personal lives and then shared their writings with other students and adults by publishing their poems and stories. Young girls in Sisters spoke openly about teenage sexuality, personal relationships, and eating disorders and then created informational collages and posters to communicate their ideas to other middle school students. The Street Team connected music and media to issues of violence to respond to the needs of their peers and neighbors for a more peaceful community. Ninth grade Shakespearean actors sought to generate conversations among students through their interpretation of roles within *A Midsummer Night's Dream*.

In these instances, group actions translated into youth activism at multiple levels. Collectively, students identified problems and sought to address them, a widely-agreed-upon goal of service-learning and youth leadership initiatives. Through projects, students enacted key elements of activism:

- *Issues*—exploring social justice and personal identity issues
- *Voice*—making decisions collectively about project design and activities
- *Audience*—impacting others through their work as individuals and group members
- *Change*—envisioning and working toward new possibilities for themselves, their schools and their community

In so doing, the students practiced the understandings and skills that leaders who are activists need to get things done in complex political and organizational settings, including asserting their own capacities, working with adults as active partners, explaining concepts to others, building problem-solving dialogs, and resolving issues through meetings with teachers and other students.

Fourth, middle and high school students took on activist roles in legacy projects that were developed separate from the traditional school framework. The Street Team met on Saturdays, and these youth saw their role as influencing the wider neighborhood community. The Writing and Acting Club encouraged young people to express themselves by writing about self-selected topics, not teacher-assigned topics. Sisters talked about issues that students say were rarely discussed in their classes. It is also interesting that two of the legacy projects in which youth took on activist roles—the Writing and Acting Club and Sisters—were developed by college undergraduates who were in the schools only one or two afternoons a week, not by teacher certification candidates who were in the schools all day for the entire school year.

As teacher educators and youth leadership developers, we need to recognize that youth activism can involve going against the grain of young peoples' everyday educational experiences. Letting students set forth their own concerns and agendas for change also means letting them question and critique why those concerns and agendas are not always addressed within the regular school day. We also need to consider how time spent within the dominant culture of the school blocks rather than fosters innovative thinking about new roles for youth. We must do more within our teacher preparation programs to help prospective teachers and tutors deal with the inhibitors and enablers of school change.

Finally, recent efforts to reform education have stressed prescribed courses and stricter standards based on clearly articulated "knowledge bases" for beginning teachers and secondary students. Considerable emphasis is placed on what new teachers and students must be able to do in the classroom as measured by specific performance outcome indicators. Such efforts to rationalize learning say little about the inherent power of working with adolescents outside of formally structured classroom settings. In responding to reform, we must not limit our field of vision such that many potentially creative and empowering ways for certification candidates to work with youth are deemphasized or never tried at all. We must welcome contexts for learning—projects, people, issues—where teachers guide youth to work as activists for change.

It is from this standpoint of teacher leadership and youth activism that the most telling impacts of legacy projects as a change process may be found. Spiraling outward, like the ripples caused by a rock that is tossed into the middle of a deep calm pool, legacies will affect the attitudes and behaviors of everyone involved in them. Some teachers and some youths will carry on the ideas and insights they have gained. Then, unlike the impact of the rock in the pond, the ripples created will not lose their intensity as they move farther away from the initial point of impact. Rather, like radio waves from a far-off cosmic event, legacies will travel onward at an accelerating rate of speed, continuing to change the ways in which teachers relate to students, youth relate to teachers, and schools organize themselves to promote learning and teaching.

Acknowledgments

The authors express thanks to the students and teachers at Springfield Central High School, Central Academy, and Chestnut Accelerated Middle School for the Visual and Performing Arts, members of the 1996–97 class of 180 Days in Springfield, and students from the TEAMS Tutoring Project for their contributions to the legacy projects and to this essay.

References

Britzman, D. 1991. *Practice makes practice: A critical study of learning to teach.* Albany: State University of New York Press.

Carnegie Council on Adolescent Development. 1989. *Turning points: Preparing American youth for the 21st century.* Washington, D.C.: Carnegie Foundation.

Goodlad, J. 1984. *A place called school: Prospects for the future.* New York: McGraw-Hill.

Johnson, S. M. 1990. *Teachers at work: Achieving success in our schools.* New York: Basic Books.

Lakes, R. D. 1996. *Youth development and critical education: The promise of democratic action.* Albany: State University of New York Press.

McNeil, L. 1986. *Contradictions of control: School structure and school knowledge.* New York: Routledge.

Shor, I. 1996. *When students have power: Negotiating authority in a critical pedagogy.* Chicago: University of Chicago Press.

Chapter 11

Empowering Teacher Education Students through Service Learning: A Case Study

Carol W. Kinsley

Teacher educators have been talking about service learning since it was embraced as a methodology in K–12 classrooms in the late 1980s. An ongoing and central question has been: "How can we advance the understanding of service as both an instructional methodology and a strategy for educational reform?" Although teachers have used community service experiences for generations as a "nice," extracurricular thing for students to do on occasion, integration of service learning more fully and effectively into the curriculum, so as to enhance students' academic understanding and their social and personal growth, remains a complex, challenging issue.

Because service learning is implemented by teachers, a logical response has been to focus on teacher education for preservice students, teachers in service, and those pursuing graduate education degrees. The wheels of change grind slowly in colleges and universities, but during the 1990s many schools of education began to incorporate service learning into their teacher education programs. The change was due largely to the interest of faculty members who saw in service learning both a powerful pedagogy and an important path for school reform. Examples of how service learning has become part of teacher education include situations for undergraduate students in tutoring, microteaching experiences, service integrated into methods courses, and continuing education courses about service learning.

Based on the theories of John Dewey, Ralph Tyler, Hilda Taba, and Paulo Friere and on actual experiences with teachers, research has been conducted on K–12 service learning to investigate the rationale, process, and results of integrating service learning into curriculum. Several of these studies have focused on the organizational structures and the active, thematic learning recommended by middle school reform, and a number of these investigations have concluded that service learning is an ideal teaching strategy. Specifically, the research has produced examples of how teachers and students identified needs in their communities, researched issues, established themes, reviewed ways in which these themes could be connected to learning objectives, built a repertoire of activities, reflected on these activities, then evaluated the unit. As I wrote in 1992:

> In the development and implementation of the service project, staff were given the opportunity to make decisions about the content and service activities for their school. One teacher felt she had been given "permission" to teach students in a way that reaches them. . . .
>
> With learning objectives identified and connections with community organizations made, service projects became activities with students actively engaged in learning about areas such as the environment, the elderly, health/safety issues, the homeless and hungry, and citizenship through hands-on lessons. Curriculum content was learned in a lively manner, usually in group experiences both in the school and in the community. (Kinsley, 1992, 42)

The result of this kind of work and research is that we are beginning to move in our understanding of service learning from the theoretical to real examples of how to bring this kind of learning alive for students—from kindergarten through graduate school. One of several teacher education programs that recognized the value of service learning and began to explore ways to incorporate it into the program takes place at the School of Education of the University of Massachusetts at Amherst. As a manifestation of the school's interest, *Equity and Excellence*, the School of Education's journal, used community-service learning (CSL) as its theme in the September 1993 issue. Also, on reviewing a doctoral dissertation about how to integrate community service learning into middle school education in the 1990s, one UMass education professor suggested that community service learning could be the "smoking gun of education reform." Reading how teachers used service learning to create situations for the middle school students to become actively engaged and involved in their subject areas and at the same time develop relationships with others, the professor recognized elements of education reform when service learning was used as a methodology. Other professors in the University of Massachusetts Secondary Teacher Education Program (STEP) created a course, Tutoring Enrichment and Assistance Models with Schools

(TEAMS), in which students learned how to teach by tutoring students in sixth to twelfth grade schools; they also attended a seminar on analyzing their teaching and understanding the schools and communities in which they were placed. In addition, the Integrated Day Program (kindergarten through fifth grade teacher education program within the School of Education) incorporated a community service-learning course in its continuing education program for area teachers earning a master's degree.

Based on discussions with professors from STEP, a grant proposal was prepared and submitted by the Community Service Learning Center in 1994 to the local Community Foundation of Western Massachusetts to support a pilot course on community service-learning for graduate students. At the time, STEP was undergoing significant organizational changes. Thus, it wasn't until 1996–97 that the course found a home as an alternative to microteaching, an early teaching experience taking place prior to student-teaching practicums in the sequence of programs for graduate students enrolled in the teacher certification program. In all, nine students and six cooperating teachers participated in the pilot effort. To demonstrate the meaning of service learning as a teaching methodology, this chapter will analyze and summarize the content of the course, the process of integrating service learning into curriculum, the graduate students' experiences in fifth through twelfth grade classrooms, and their reactions to the seminar and their placements.

The syllabus described the course, Workshop in Education: Integrating Community Based Learning into the Curriculum (615H), as one that provides students with the theory and practice of integrating community service learning into teaching and learning throughout the K–12 curriculum. Participants learned how service experiences can enhance learning in all curriculum and program areas in schools by bringing active and reflective learning to students and by developing the school community.

Participants also gained insights and learned methods of how CSL, once integrated into curriculum, can advance such school improvement initiatives as inclusion, multicultural education, active learning, team teaching, thematic curriculum, flexible scheduling, student-centered learning, and community involvement. The seminar students explored recent research that shows how students learn and clarifies the elements necessary to successful school restructuring. In the process, they gained an understanding of how CSL supports the constructivist theory of education.

Students were required to complete all reading and writing assignments; work with a teacher implementing CSL for 60 to 80 hours to understand how to use CSL as a teaching and learning method and to assist the teacher in CSL development; develop a service-learning curriculum unit for future use or implement a unit (each unit will include authentic pedagogy, school organizational capacity, and the interaction with the community partner); and keep a journal throughout the course. Based on articles and videos about teachers who had used service learning in all content areas, the students explored how service learning affects teaching, learning, a school culture, and the community. Through their school placements, the students were able to test the service-learning theory by working with a cooperating teacher, presenting lessons, and helping implement service-learning activities. Students learned the various ways that teachers use service experiences in the classroom—for instance, by teaching others content areas (cross-age instruction), tutoring, and integrating service experiences into curriculum and program areas. In its pure sense, service learning, when integrated into "regular" learning, was seen by the students as a useful, effective teaching tool.

The purpose and value of using reflection was reinforced throughout the seminar as students kept journals and wrote reflective papers. This helped them to understand their experience. As one seminar student observed, "The learning comes not just from doing but from stepping back and observing yourself doing, and thinking about the experience." This realization was shared by other students. (The unexpected value was to show how the journals and reflective papers helped further develop the understanding of the meaning of service learning in teacher education programs.)

The seminar students also realized that as young people contribute to and care about others, they learn to care for themselves. Their caring extended beyond cognitive learning to supporting the affective, social, and personal development of young people. Through an assigned paper, the class quickly grasped the holistic nature of community service learning used as a methodology and responded enthusiastically to its potential for teachers and students.

Seminar Students' Initial Reaction to Service Learning

An initial reaction of the students in the seminar was that community service learning is as good and simple as apple pie and motherhood, a process through which secondary students can do good work, feel good about it, and contribute to the community. A win-win for students and the community. Growing beyond this simplistic view, however, seminar participants perceived the potential complexities of a service-learning activity. Through discussion, the class came to realize that the scope of service learning can be extensive—that some of the community needs and issues that become part of community service learning have broader implications. They give teachers opportunities to involve students in examining real issues that can change schools, communities, and their own self-perception.

For example, the seminar students realized that by having their students explore an issue such as homelessness and hunger, they would have to decide how simple or complex they would want to make the experience and curriculum unit. Feeding the homeless at a soup kitchen, for instance, could be considered a simple act of charity or a starting point for a discussion on the meaning and result of homelessness and hunger for individuals and communities. Ultimately, students might become advocates for those in need.

Simply put, the seminar students came to realize and understand early on the complex issues and dynamics involved in implementing community service learning, anticipating the implications addressed by Joseph Kahne and Joel Westheimer in their article "In the Service of What? The Politics of Service Learning" (1996). The article is based on a year-long study of two dozen K–12 teachers who took part in a university-sponsored effort to promote service learning. They examined the underlying means and ends of these service-learning activities by raising the question, "Is the purpose of service learning to affect change or provide charitable acts?" A lively discussion ensued in the seminar class, based on the students' classroom experience and their response to the questions, insights, and analysis put forth by Kahne and Westheimer.

Rationale for Using Service Learning

Early in the seminar, the class also discussed the question, "Why should we make the effort to use service learning?" Used as a teaching methodology, it can mean extra time organizing the experience with the community, developing curriculum based on students' interests rather than making unilateral decisions, and guiding 25 learning plans rather than developing one lecture. My first response was, simply, that students receive a better education with CSL—they learn better, more broadly, and more deeply than in the classroom alone. Second, it changes students as human beings. What did the seminar students think? The students shared their feelings on how their own service experiences had affected and redirected their lives. One student articulated her thoughts in a way that surprised me, as she is a graduate of a very respected high school with excellent grades and is very responsible and engaged. She wrote:

> When I went to high school, most of my peers and I felt that school was to be suffered through until we entered "real life," and any meaning that we might find for ourselves, or any personal growth that occurred, would be through an extracurricular activity, such as a drama club, or through meeting friends and socializing. We were forced to go to school, and it was a vehicle to go to college, and while we were there we could find ways to have fun on the periphery. There was not any CSL in any classes in my school.
>
> CSL is a powerful tool to change this feeling. As was demonstrated in the video [a review of an elementary, middle, and high school using service learning as a methodology to bring about change and build community in their school], CSL projects can bring the school together in ways that are meaningful for students, which connect their daily lives to the curriculum, create multiple opportunities for success for diverse learners, and create opportunities for students to actively contribute to their community, therefore having a sense of accomplishment that is not often offered in high school.
>
> CSL is a good pedagogy: it creates opportunities for parental and community involvement in the curriculum, and for students to actively engage, think critically and solve problems, and be authentically assessed through the process of serving and the products that the students create (such as an educational presentation about water testing). CSL encourages students to work cooperatively, and encourages students to share their strengths instead of finding short cuts to a good grade. . . .
>
> CSL is a powerful educational tool that must be handled correctly for all students to ask critical questions, solve problems, and gain skills that will be used for a lifetime. Through working cooperatively to address real issues and addressing inequities in society, students will no longer feel that school is something to suffer through until graduation to "real life." They will be living it. (Wohlleb)[1]

In these few short paragraphs, this seminar student described how she felt service learning could have enriched her high school education, transforming it from boring to engaging, from "something to be suffered through" to a lively and authentic learning experience. We know that researchers and theorists are telling us to change our schools to meet the needs of our students. Here, we have a university student, not far from her high school years, suggesting a way to alleviate the boredom, the malaise, the waste of years, to bring meaning to learning.

Response to Recent Research

The seminar readings from Fred Newman and Gary Wehlage's *Successful School Restructuring* (1995) introduced students to research that outlines critical elements of school restructuring. Newman and Wehlage summarized recent studies and concluded that the common characteristics of successful school restructuring consisted of (1) student-centered learning, (2) authentic pedagogy, (3) the organization of the school, whether it represents hierarchical or inclusive decision making, and (4) external support.

The seminar students were asked to describe how CSL supports these criteria. Based on their review of the research and classroom experience, the students concluded that service learning could be a useful strategy to support student-centered learning, authentic learning, strong organizational supports, and external connections with the community.

One seminar student who worked with eleventh grade English classes reflected on the connection and responded with the following:

> Basically, they [Newman and Wehlage] are attempting to articulate a brand of learning and teaching that requires engagement of students and teachers in the material and process of learning. It is learning by doing and learning by thinking about what we are doing. The manner in which CSL can fit into this model seems self-evident. CSL asks students and teachers to re-engage with the curriculum through action and reflection upon that action. It asks teachers to ask students to make use of their knowledge in the world. And it sets a standard for learning that reflects an in-depth understanding, through experience, of what is learned.
>
> Because CSL by its nature includes others from a wider community than just the classroom, it encourages the kind of communication and support that Newman and Wehlage mean by external support. Ideally, CSL challenges the school organizational capacity as well by including teachers, students, administrators and staff from various disciplines. CSL should have repercussions for each of the areas of school restructuring because its successful implementation requires making different kinds of connections between learners and knowledge; students and teachers; teachers and content areas; teachers, students and others within the school; and, most clearly, between the school and the larger community.
>
> . . . Some of the issues the authors seem to be addressing are the relationship between the student and the knowledge, and the relationship between the teacher and the student. In both cases I would use the words engagement and connection to describe the quality that they aspire to in these schools. Yet, if not properly implemented, I can imagine a CSL project that becomes more activity than action and is more about product than process. . . . I am concerned that some CSL projects may not be engaging the students in the learning in a different manner (student-centered) when it seems to be imposed

and if it does not include a reflective element. I am not certain, but I see where there is room for students to have the same kind of alienation from [a service] project that they have from certain books they are asked to read. If CSL is to break through that alienation, we teachers are going to have to really struggle with issues of how to manage the different voices and needs which arise when one begins to include circles of the larger community in a project.

How can we balance the learning with the service? I fear the learning gets lost more easily than the service and my heart is with the learner as the priority. I see how these issues can develop and hope only to be able to remain alert to them as I develop and implement my own projects in my teaching career. (Madeloni)

Another graduate student assigned to a high school community service-learning class wrote:

CSL fosters both authentic pedagogy and student learning through necessitating analysis, the understanding of disciplinary concepts, and elaborate discourse. CSL experiences are interdisciplinary in nature and require the ability to problem solve, to consider alternatives, and to communicate orally and in writing the objective and rationale behind the service and students' reflections on providing the service. CSL also requires the ability to discourse openly about problems and their possible solutions.

The risk of requiring students to reproduce knowledge is reduced in CSL. Interactions with other human beings are inescapably individual. When providing service, there is no set knowledge that the students can regurgitate back to the teacher. Students construct knowledge on top of a base built of their prior personal and academic experiences. As they gather the knowledge necessary for implementing the service, they participate in disciplined inquiry. . . .

It is in providing a space for students' experiences to have value beyond school that CSL can most explicitly support the elements of successful school restructuring. In order to implement and fulfill their service plans, students must "communicate ideas, produce products [and] have an impact on others." (Monette)

These comments clearly express the connection the students found between CSL and research. But the students responses went even further. Because of their exposure to theory in the seminar, practice in the classroom, and the analysis of recent education reform research, they provided insights and cautions about how to use CSL as an effective learning tool.

Renata and Geoffrey Caine have conducted research on how the brain learns and the implications of this research for learning environments. In their book *Making Connections: Teaching and the Hu-*

man Brain (1994), they describe 12 brain-based learning principles that they believe "provide guidelines for defining and selecting programs and methodologies" (199). They challenge traditional education and suggest that the "brain does not naturally separate emotions from cognition, either anatomically or perceptually. Hence, they argue, brain research challenges the belief that teaching can be separated into the cognitive, affective, and psychomotor domains" (vii). Further, their research makes them question the use of rote memorization and teaching of facts as valid instructional strategies. In fact, they write, "we have come to the conclusion that educators, by being too specific about facts to be remembered and outcomes to be produced, may inhibit students' genuine understanding and transfer of learning" (vii).

Again through discussion and their classroom experience, seminar students identified how CSL supports each of the Caines' 12 brain-based learning principles and how the connection with the principles increases the credibility of service learning as a methodology. One seminar student who worked with high school students saw them transformed from passive and disinterested observers to fully engaged participants in service activities. She observed:

> Through planning and implementing service projects, students learn about the people they serve, they learn professional skills required to coordinate a service project, they learn about themselves and their own leadership skills, and they learn about each other, and gain respect for the accomplishments the class has done. The CSL class fosters a type of learning that is not often recognized as valuable in the context of traditional academics, but is specifically valued by brain-based learning theorists.
>
> They [students] work harder, learn more and achieve greater results when they are setting up a project which they are invested in and feel happy about doing. They greatly resist any activity in which they feel stifled, or they do not understand the significance of. The power of the class clearly draws from the rapport that is built among the students and the teacher through creating projects that students feel good about.
>
> The brain works best when facts and skills are embedded in natural, spatial memory, and enhanced by challenge. Students in the CSL class learn their most important lessons through experience. They learn about the world and about themselves by creating challenging situations and seeing what works well. Students learn about professionalism and identity in a way that cannot be taught in a traditional class. I believe this is the most powerful learning that the students gain.
>
> . . . [W]hen seen through the lens of brain-based learning theory, [the students] learn in a deep way that is embedded in their memory and feels

"natural," because it is how the brain functions best. As they learn about the world and about themselves, their brains work better, which will carry over into other classes and into their ability to solve problems and address situations in all other parts of their lives. (Wohlleb)

Other seminar students noted the way CSL provided students with a sense of meaning about what they are doing and learning and connected them to their environment, consistent with the Caines' principle 3, which states that the search for meaning is innate and that there is a consequential, automatic need to act on our environment. CSL also involves students' emotions, supporting principle 5, which suggests that emotions are critical to patterning and that it is impossible to isolate the cognitive and affective domains in a learning situation. From their experiences, the students observed that CSL lends itself to a holistic view of student learning—affective and cognitive— and that through the critical use of reflection it allows the students to process feelings and emotions as well as academic content.

School Placements: Testing the Theory and Foundations

As described earlier, all of the seminar students were matched with teachers who were implementing some aspect of service learning. In the placements, they were required to teach minilessons and assist the cooperating teacher with organizing the service-learning activities. As a byproduct of the seminar, they tested the theory provided in the seminar and they experienced the complexities, issues, and other challenges of service learning in practice.

Although there were nine students in the course, space limits the discussion here to two placements, one each in fifth and eleventh grade classrooms. The thoughts shared in the students' journals and reflections further illustrate the importance of connecting real experiences with the theory and practice learned in the classroom.

Fifth Grade Placement

Michele Hebert, the fifth grade teacher at Liberty Elementary School, has used community service learning as a methodology since the late 1980s and was a pioneer in the development of CSL in the elementary schools. To learn and reinforce regular curriculum and certain leadership and social skills, her fifth grade students participate in two service activities: with the intergenerational Team Leaders, and with younger students in the Buddy Reading Programs. The Team Leaders, six to eight in number from a neighborhood retirement home for well elderly, meet with the fifth graders biweekly and participate in a wide range of activities that correspond to curriculum topics. Buddy Reading consists of a partnership with a special needs class whose pupils are younger than the "big" fifth grade students. They meet every Friday at 2 p.m. and are paired one on one. The fifth graders read to or share an activity with the younger students with a true spirit of giving and caring.

The seminar student described the fifth grade and its school partners as representing the "epitome of a safe learning environment . . . where the fifth graders feel they have a job to do. They are helping the special needs students—liking them is just a by-product." She cites that the students are aware of the change in their behaviors toward their reading buddies, quoting one fifth grade student who wrote, "I think more teachers should start buddy reading. . . .They should start the program so that other kids won't make fun of special needs children but help them." The seminar student continued:

> I think the level of self-understanding . . . indicated by this student's writing, alone, indicates the depth of possibilities for social change that a CSL program offers. . . . But, the benefits of a CSL-based approach to teaching goes further. The CSL experience provides a foundation or reference point for all areas of teaching. A teacher's job is to help students connect to learning material. In a diverse student body . . . the CSL program becomes a common denominator—something everyone in the class has a relationship to, something everyone in the class cares about.

This same seminar student observed that the class's interaction with the Team Leaders produced an environment in which the fifth graders' "genuine feelings, their caring and concern for the Team Leaders, cause them to truly apply themselves to any task which might be connected to the elders." The seminar student went on to describe a lesson she designed on poetry, which was focused on the Team Leaders, first as the subjects for the poems, and second to motivate the students to stay involved as their poems would be collected in a book and given to the elders. Her comment, "Connecting the poem writing to a meaningful end like publishing, illustrating and reading for the team leaders—people outside the classroom—is a huge, huge motivator. It made my job easy."

The first time the seminar student met with the teacher and the class, she observed the student-centered nature of the classroom and recounted,

I, as an adult, expected to talk with [the teacher] to create a plan, an agenda. I expected to be told about the students and what they are doing and I expected her to frame out what she expected of me in relation to the project . . . I would be handling. Instead, she had the students tell me about the project. More, the students told me about many of their projects. The students told me how they learn. They told me how the teachers teach them. . . . They told me, if possible, not to come to work with them on Mondays because it's a bad day for them . . . they are too unsettled from the weekend on Mondays but by Tuesday they are more settled. The teacher had one of the students write the classroom schedule out for me.

I felt so welcome. The students are so honest and willing to share. Why did I expect them to be shy? Why would I think that the young man who wrote the schedule for me would consider it a burden to have this task? Instead of a burden he saw it as an honor. . . . The teacher seems to find the strengths of the students and builds them into classroom management. Another student has outstanding knowledge of the computer, so he runs the computer department. He oversees computer use.

What might I take from here and translate into the middle or high school environment? (Killion)

Overall, her experience with the fifth grade students and their teacher helped her develop a vision of herself as a teacher. She said, "I find when asked to participate in teaching assignments, I'm thinking experiential learning. It's making teaching exciting and challenging for me."

Eleventh Grade Placement

Another seminar student was assigned to work with eleventh grade students in English classes taught by Bettie Hallen at the High School of Science and Technology. She worked with three different classes, gaining input from them about their service-learning activities, guiding them, and helping them organize their service experiences. Two classes participated in activities with elders and the Olympic Specialty Hospital. One class worked on a citywide project. Initially, she struggled with organizational issues, schedules, and the problem of how to use these experiences to enhance learning. The result of her efforts was several interactions between the students and the residents of the two institutions that heightened her awareness and belief in the value of providing opportunities for students to participate in what she terms "the human connection."

For instance, as she observed her students relating to the elders, she recounts, "[W]atching the five young men with the two older men, watching them listen to what the men said and laugh with them, watching them be respectful and proud and encouraged: there are just so many gifts being passed back and forth that there is no saying who benefits most."

Her final observations provided insight into the complexity of service learning and into what her limited time in the eleventh grade classroom taught her:

> I move so cautiously into CSL though I do not want to. I want to believe that people helping each other is enough. And it is so much. But it isn't enough. It is a beginning but we need to attend closely to where we are going and why to carry it through. We must proceed with hope for the power of human connections but we must attend to the nature and meaning of those connections. . . . In order to make CSL meaningful we need to examine how we give, and what we give. We also need to be alert to how giving is understood in the society as a whole.
>
> Working in CSL has led me to consider everything I do as a teacher and how it connects to real meanings in the world. Education is about how we make meaning and teaching children to engage the world in a manner which allows them to comprehend the meaning, understand its derivation, and participate in making meaning. . . . Done well CSL communicates about taking part in one's community and being active within democracy; it communicates that it matters to understand problems and to participate in problem-solving, and often volunteerism is not going to be enough. . . . It matters to teach children that connections matter. (Madeloni)

These insights from seminar students' experience of the two classes help us understand what happens when service learning becomes part of a teacher's "toolbox." Further, they help us understand the meaning of integrating service learning in teacher education programs. The seminar students not only gained insights into using service learning in the context of the "real world of teaching," they became more reflective about themselves as individuals and teachers.

What Have We Learned? Implications for CSL as a Pedagogy

The following conclusions can be drawn from the seminar. First, implementing service learning is more complex than it initially appears and certainly more so than implementing traditional extracurricular community service. Second, the reactions of the nine seminar students to the seminar and the placements reflected an excitement and value in using service learning as a teaching strategy. Recurring themes throughout their discussions and papers pointed to service-learning activities as ways to implement student-centered learning, increase students' motivation for learning content, increase opportunities for students to become involved in understanding their communities and to effect change within them, and build more positive relationships—with other students in their classes and within the school and with their teachers and other community members—providing a vehicle for positive social interaction.

Clearly, the seminar students observed a difference in the classroom learning when the K–12 students were truly invested in the service activities and when their work was teacher-directed. Their interest, involvement, and motivation were heightened when they had input. By contrast, the seminar students noted that when ideas and direction came from outside, there were instances of resistance and frustration.

Over and over the seminar students expressed the importance of relationships that were byproducts of the service experiences. They cited how they observed the relationships with the community partners, relationships as motivators, providing the impetus for learning academics, but also more about others and self. They saw how developing an "authentic product," such as a book of poetry for the elderly, provided motivation in developing the poetry as well as providing a book that reflected quality, one in which they felt pride.

Certainly challenges surfaced. Although the seminar students said the seminar was meaningful and they gained a deep appreciation for using service learning as a pedagogy, they identified challenges which were generally organizational. Often schedules needed to be changed owing to illness, inclement weather, or an emergency at the school or service site. (However, as one seminar student noted, her cooperating teacher would make a positive learning experience even out of a schedule change.) They also recognized the need for specific, concrete planning for preparation, the activity, and timelines to alleviate frustrations and ensure successful completion of the activities. Some of the seminar students' journal entries indicate their concern that the community partners might not uphold their end of the partnership, a natural reaction when a relationship built on prior working together and trust has not been established. One journal entry stated, "part of designing these projects has to be [defining] your community resources and making sure that they are of the kind to be consistent enough to really help while flexible enough to allow for the vagaries of high school life" (Madeloni).

Another challenge was to give more attention to the seminar students' placements to ensure both student and cooperating teacher had common expectations and understanding of their roles. Even though roles had been defined, it became quite clear that the cooperating teachers needed to gather for an orientation with the seminar students, and together they needed to outline for each other their expectations and roles. Since the seminar students were just beginning their teacher certification program and microteaching provided them with their first experience in front of a group of students, they needed support and guidance from the cooperating teacher.

Dan Goleman, in an interview for *Educational Leadership* (see Pool, 1997), expressed the importance of understanding emotional intelligence and outlined what he feels are its five dimensions. It is clear that these dimensions are reinforced and supported by service learning. They include self-awareness, general ability to handle emotions, motivation, empathy, and social skills. Of empathy Goleman stated, "Empathy is the brake on human cruelty. It is what keeps civility alive in society" (14). The service-learning situations described and observed by the seminar students clearly support the strong rationale for using service learning to help teachers reach their students and for the young people to have a viable means for the development of these five dimensions. Certainly, Goleman's research gives added impetus to the use of service learning in schooling and to its inclusion in teacher education. He states that social-emotional programs should become "integrated into the curriculum and the life of the school. . . . They do best when they go for the long term and when teachers are well trained" (14).

The seminar students reflected a genuine excitement in finding a methodology that supports values they care about and that provides students with academic challenges. Although building a partnership with a community entity increases the complexity of implementing service learning as curriculum, the seminar students endorsed the partnership idea because of the additional motivation and opportunities to apply classroom skills. Understanding how to build these bridges with community partners to provide appropriate learning situations and to integrate the experience into curriculum are techniques that need to become part of a teacher's repertoire of teaching strategies.

A concluding memo from one seminar student included the thought, "I learned more than I yet know. Thank you." It is a statement that reflects the synergy, serendipitous nature, and power of CSL as a pedagogy, the unknown of mixing curriculum development with relationships, building on experiences, meeting real needs in the community, and being open to the possibilities!

Acknowledgments

The author wants to thank Professors Richard Clark, Patrick Sullivan, Robert Maloy, and the late Byrd Jones, all from the School of Education, University of Massachusetts at Amherst, for their encouragement and support in the development of this seminar and the ultimate placement of the course as an alternative to microteaching. Rachel Bent acted as a graduate assistant throughout the year and helped make the necessary connections between teachers and students. Her consistent contact with the seminar students enabled us to monitor the progress of the seminar and the placements and is deeply appreciated.

The author also thanks Superintendent Peter J. Negroni, Springfield Public Schools; President Linda Wilson, Springfield Education Association, who sanctioned the project in the Springfield Public Schools; and especially the teachers who acted as cooperating teachers and agreed to participate in this pilot project.

Last, a thank you is extended to the Community Foundation of Western Massachusetts that provided the funding for this pilot project at the School of Education, University of Massachusetts at Amherst, and the Board of Directors of the Community Service Learning Center, who approved of and supported the endeavor.

Notes

1. The material used to chronicle the impressions of the seminar students was drawn from the journals and papers submitted by Candice Killion, Aimee Monette, Barbara Madeloni, and Beth Wohlleb. Each has given permission for the use of their reflective thoughts and reactions. Their very different experiences in the classroom provided us with valuable insights into how theory and practice combine to enrich teaching and learning through service learning. Their sincere commitment to teaching bodes well for their future students.

References

Caine, R., and G. Caine. 1994. *Making connections: Teaching and the human brain*. Menlo Park, Calif.: Addison-Wesley.

Kahne, J., and J. Westheimer. 1996. In the service of what? The politics of service learning. *Phi Delta Kappan*, 77(9): 593–599.

Kinsley, C. 1992. *A case study: The integration of community service learning into the curriculum by an interdisciplinary team of teachers at an urban middle school*. Ph.D. diss., University of Massachusetts, Amherst.

Newman, F., and G. Whelage. 1995. *Successful school restructuring: A report to the public and educators by the center on the organization and restructuring of schools*. Madison: Board of Regents of the University of Wisconsin System.

Pool, C. 1997. Up with emotional health: An interview with Dan Goleman. *Educational Leadership*, 54(8): 12–14.

Chapter 12

Going Beyond Service

Curtis Ogden

Go to the People,
Live with them,
Learn from them,
Love them.
Start with what they know,
Build with what they have.

And with the best leaders
When the work is done
   the task accomplished
The people will say,
"We have done this ourselves."
                    —Lao Tse

We come to be who we are through conversation with others.
                    —Gregory Baum

For the past four years I have been involved in developing and facilitating a volunteer community service program for teenagers living in and around Ithaca, New York. Though this initiative is supported by funds from Learn and Serve America, I have been reluctant to use the term *service learning* to describe it. In talking with others, I have found service to be a difficult term to define, especially when considering concepts such as volunteerism, activism, and social action. Having participated in a number of conferences and meetings with other practitioners, I have listened to many debates about what constitutes community service. Ultimately, many of these conversations seem to reduce service to a rather conventional notion, such as picking up garbage or talking with senior citizens. Placing such limits on the concept of service constrains the scope of certain service-learning programs and the imagination of the young people in them. I spend much of my time trying to expand service to incorporate new ideas, perspectives, and energy. Many of the young people with whom I have worked have commented on the cold and institutional ring of the term *service learning*. "It's more than that," they often say. Indeed it is. Perhaps no words can accurately capture the true potential of what we have dubbed *service learning*. Let me suggest, however, that our actions will speak even louder and more meaningfully if we set our sights beyond service.

Many of the lessons I have learned and applied to the development of the Learning Web service program derive from my experiences working with youth living on the streets of Harare, Zimbabwe. Following my undergraduate studies, I participated in an overseas development program through an organization called Visions in Action. I was sent to Zimbabwe, where I worked as a volunteer with two local organizations devoted to improving the circumstances of impoverished communities. I came to view my work at that time as having more to do with community development than service. This distinction began with my academic training at the University of Michigan, where I studied cultural anthropology. My studies in international development and applied ethnology advocated a holistic and participatory outlook on what is often viewed as service aimed at helping those in need.

The field of international development has long suffered from a paternalistic and patronizing approach to working with *un-, under-,* and *less* developed communities. The belief that Western nations should serve as a benchmark for so-called "Third World" development (modernization theory) is now popularly recognized as self-serving, corrupt, and culturally inappropriate. Increasingly, development efforts acknowledge and respect indigenous capacities and the necessity of engaging targeted populations in decision making to facilitate meaningful social change. In other words, more people now ask the important first question, "Development for whom and for what?"

My experience with a grassroots organization called Streets Ahead in Harare introduced me in a practical way to participatory development. The aim of Streets Ahead is to assist children who find themselves living or working on the streets of Zimbabwe's capital city. The staff begin with the belief that the rights and personhood of each and every child should be respected. When I joined the organization, Linda Dube, a Zimbabwean sociologist and Streets Ahead staff member, had spent the previous three years with the children on their turf, getting to know them as individuals and building relationships of love, trust, and confidence. This was a vital foundation for the organization's future efforts. As we wrote in our first newsletter:

> The capacity of these children to determine their own destiny has been widely underrated and undermined. The visible child in the streets should be viewed as a skillful individual who, against all odds, has developed means to survive. These children have learned behaviors appropriate to the environment in which they live and have developed a measure of independence. If they are to leave the streets and the independence they value for something "better" the children must be involved in the decision. . . . Otherwise proposed or imposed strategies are likely to fail. (Dube and Ogden, 1993, 1)

We worked with these youth and their families to procure premises for a drop-in center, to establish a recreation program, to create a dance/theater troupe, and to develop a community-based school and curriculum in one of the townships. All of this was based on the expressed needs, interests, and talents of the people themselves. Over time I came to view the street youth as not strictly needy but as having both needs and strengths. I learned to shy away from prescription and engage the participation of those with whom I was working. I also found that good intentions do not ensure positive or desirable outcomes. My identity as a white, relatively well off, American male made it difficult for some people to see past my wallet to my heart. For example, during a conversation with a young Zimbabwean man about the reasons for my being in his country, I was given the following interpretation of the word *volunteer*: a rich foreigner. Try as I might to refute this, there was no denying that my very presence often distracted others from discovering and developing their own resources. In these instances it took time and patience to get beyond appearances and build trustful relationships. Until this happened, my personal goals were frustrated. Thus, my most profound lessons abroad came not from serving but from *not* serving. It was not the process of development that called to me but dialogue with people and the constant questioning of my own assumptions.

I returned to the United States eager to apply this perspective to my work with young people and their work with others. I found my way to the Learning Web, where I was offered a position that included the responsibility of further developing a community service program for middle and high school youth. Since accepting, I have had my idealism challenged by many of the beliefs and attitudes that exist in this country about service, and perhaps even more so about service learning.

The service-learning movement has certainly gathered steam in recent years, fueled by growing concern over young people's disengagement from schools and public life. As I have seen it, youth are often viewed as being apathetic, and service is often held up as a means of reconnecting them with the world around them. In this period of renewed interest in experiential education, service is lauded as a rewarding, hands-on activity. In this age of "living democracy" it is praised as a tool for teaching civic responsibility. In the ongoing push to reform schools, it is promoted as a revitalizing agent of curricula and classrooms.

Despite all of its promise and potential, though, there is something about service learning that concerns me. It has everything to do with the lessons learned from misguided international development efforts and my own experiences in Harare. Before everyone jumps on the service-learning bandwagon, I encourage practitioners to recognize that their goal should be to go *beyond* service. To focus on the act of service is to miss the point. Fundamentally, service is a dead enterprise if we do not understand and appreciate its underlying purpose and consequences. We, too, must learn to begin with the question, "Service for whom and for what?"

Implicit in the concept of service is an element of hierarchy. As an action, service responds to a perceived imbalance. It is need-oriented. As a relationship, service manifests itself as an exchange between the server and the served. In the scope of this exchange, there is a distinction between the one who provides and the one who receives, between the one who has and the one who does not have. Given this subtle articulation of power, the manner in which the exchange takes place can be a delicate matter. When gone awry, the act of service can take on an air of loftiness that perpetuates rather than rights imbalance. Robert Coles acknowledges this danger in the service provided by teachers. In the words of one of his former mentors: "There's moral asymmetry that takes hold of us teachers too commonly—we think of ourselves as offering service to others, giving them our best, and forget . . . the service that we're receiving from our students" (Coles, 1993, 177).

In other words, it is important that accompanying our actions is a certain level of consciousness that takes us beyond the desire to help. Continuing from Coles: "What we do on behalf of others may be a big puzzle to them, perhaps because we patronize them, condescend to them, convey to them our sense of lofty *noblesse oblige,* even hector them with it, while refusing to acknowledge (to ourselves, perhaps also to them) our own purposes and reasons, and, very important, our own needs" (Coles, 1993, 177). This lack of awareness can have dire consequences, turning service upon itself, fracturing community rather than building it.

I want to stress that empowering young people to serve may not be the same as promoting the common good. It is possible to teach them about service without teaching them to respect others. There is a risk in standardizing service learning as a pedagogical tool. When we become focused on educational outcomes and development, we are seeing only a portion of the picture. At a recent conference I heard a young person talk about his experiences working at a homeless shelter for a semester. "I have learned that we need the homeless," he said passionately, "because we can learn a lot from them." By labeling people as "the homeless" it proves that we have learned very little. The crux of the experience is missed if we fail to see the humanity of those we are serving. They are not just homeless but may also be artistic, caring, and intelligent. Perhaps a parent. Furthermore, the point is not that we need homelessness to learn. We can certainly learn from it, but we do not want to preserve neediness in order to educate (or entertain) ourselves.

While I was in Zimbabwe, Streets Ahead was visited by a BBC reporter looking to do a report on street children. This rather insistent individual convinced us to introduce her to some of the young people we knew. When a meeting was arranged, some children showed up looking clean and sharp. The reporter seemed to be bothered by their appearance, questioning whether they were "really that poor." The interview did not last long, primarily because of her sudden lack of enthusiasm. Later, during a visit to one of the townships to gather "background noise" for her report, she complained that there was not enough going on to portray the impoverished nature of the setting. My colleagues and I were baffled. Her disappointment seemed to contradict what we thought was the ultimate purpose of her visit—to fight poverty. Her focus on need actually took her away from the reality and humanity of the situation and people.

Ridiculous? There is by my own observation in Ithaca and other communities a reaction of disappointment when neediness is not readily apparent. "But how can we serve?" "There isn't anything for us to do here." Can service really be that limited or limiting? Perhaps it is the missionary aspect of our culture that sets high standards for destitution. In some instances, I have actually witnessed competition for those elements of a community that are obviously needy. As schools require increasing numbers of students to do service, I worry about the rush for academic projects and photo opportunities and the impact this will have on the people and environments we aim to help. Service as a spectacle strays us from the path of real learning and social change.

The work of service learning should be about transcending labels and stereotypes. This requires a deeper understanding of service, society, and ourselves. Our emphasis should be not only on producing helpers but also on developing critical and creative thinkers and listeners. The tendency of some service-learning practitioners to place stress on "successful" projects troubles me. This may encourage and pump students up, but it does not necessarily teach them anything about real life. Just as we are reluctant to taint our heroes from history with the sordid facts of their lives, we sometimes refrain from allowing students to see failure or struggle in service, even though it is a natural part of any human endeavor. There is power in presenting young people with all of the complexity surrounding service and letting them confront difficult questions and situations. This can be the beginning of a deeper understanding of the world, or what Parker Palmer calls transcendence. "An education in transcendence prepares us to see beyond appearances into the hidden realities of life—beyond facts into truth, beyond self-interest into compassion, beyond our flagging energies and nagging despairs into the love required to renew the community of creation" (Palmer, 1993, 13). It is for this reason that my own projects are designed so that students will constantly question their motives and values and engage in a process of personal and social investigation prior to, during, and after service projects.

As my experiences in Zimbabwe and this country have proven, there is danger and shortsightedness in treating service as a finite activity. Not only is this unrealistic, but it misses the point and is potentially discriminatory. Service for individual edification and self-esteem is shallow. To transcend this, service learning must move into considerations of the bigger picture, taking action in a world that is interconnected. This means not simply treating someone's hunger by feeding them but respecting their humanity and considering what we all share. It means considering the root of the hunger and always thinking about why we are engaged in service, what brought us here and where we hope to go. We should not strive for the ends of personal gain through action but for rootedness in the ongoing challenge of building healthy relationships with others and our environment. It is then that service learning will be living up to its potential and actively engaging young people in the work of social change.

References

Coles, R. 1993. *The call of service: A witness to idealism.* Boston: Houghton Mifflin Company.

Dube, L., and C. Ogden. 1993. *News from the streets.* Vol. 1. Harare, Zimbabwe: Streets Ahead.

Palmer, P. 1993. *To know as we are known: Education as a spiritual journey.* San Francisco: HarperCollins.

Index

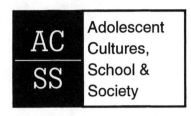

General Editors: Joseph & Linda DeVitis

As schools struggle to redefine and restructure themselves, they need to be cognizant of the new realities of adolescents. Thus, this series of monographs and textbooks is committed to depicting the variety of adolescent cultures that exist in today's post-industrial societies. It is intended to be a primarily qualitative research, practice, and policy series devoted to contextual interpretation and analysis that encompasses a broad range of interdisciplinary critique. In addition, this series will seek to provide a pragmatic, pro-active response to the current backlash of conservatism that continues to dominate political discourse, practice, and policy. This series seeks to address issues of curriculum theory and practice; multicultural education; aggression and violence; the media and arts; school dropouts; homeless and runaway youth; alienated youth; at-risk adolescent populations; family structures and parental involvement; and race, ethnicity, class, and gender studies.

Send proposals and manuscripts to the General Editors at:

Joseph & Linda DeVitis
Binghamton University
Dept. of Education & Human Development
Binghamton, NY 13902